Spiritual Maturity

Spiritual Maturity
RICHARD MAYHUE

While this book is intended for the reader's personal enjoyment and profit, it is also designed for group study. A personal and group study guide is located at the end of the text.

VICTOR BOOKS

A DIVISION OF SCRIPTURE PRESS PUBLICATIONS INC.
USA CANADA ENGLAND

Unless otherwise indicated, Scripture quotations are from the *New American Standard Bible,* © the Lockman Foundation 1960, 1962, 1963, 1968, 1971, 1972, 1973, 1975, 1977. Others are from the *Holy Bible, New International Version*® (NIV). Copyright © 1973, 1978, 1984 by International Bible Society. Used by permission of Zondervan Publishing House.

Copyediting: Carole Streeter, Barbara Williams
Cover Design: Scott Rattray
Cover Photo: Viesti Associates

Library of Congress Cataloging-in-Publication Data

Mayhue, Richard.
    Spiritual maturity / by Richard Mayhue.
      p.   cm.
    ISBN 0-89693-887-5
    1. Spiritual life. I. Title.
BV4501.2.M429   1992
248.4 – dc20   92-476
                                         CIP

---

1 2 3 4 5 6 7 8 9 10 Printing/Year 96 95 94 93 92

CONTENTS

To
Iain Michael Carson
With Your Grandfather's Prayers
That You Will Grow Up to
Honor Christ
with Holiness of Life, a Pure Love,
and Unceasing Spiritual Service
Which Marked Your Biblical Namesakes.
2 Corinthians 7:1

When the heav'ns shall ring
And the angels sing
At Thy coming to victory,
Let Thy voice call me home,
Saying, "Yet there is room—
There is room at My side for thee."
My heart shall rejoice, Lord Jesus,
When Thou comest and callest for me!'

INTRODUCTION

Four men preparing for ministry at The Master's Seminary and I invested several hours a week together throughout an entire semester focusing on spirituality. Our discipleship lab worked through a highly recommended book written by a well-known Christian. But much to our surprise, the author never defined what he meant by spirituality, even though the word appeared prominently in the title.

Because this omission struck us as serious but probably all too common, we spent the remaining time searching the Scriptures to determine the biblical meaning of spirituality. We settled on this working definition after weeks of lively inquiry and discussion. *above reproach* *maturity*

Christian spirituality involves growing to be like God in character and conduct, by personal submission to the transforming work of God's Spirit and God's Word.

1 Rom 12:2

Discussions in the first nine chapters of this book—*God's Plan*—will highlight every aspect of our definition. The last four chapters will focus on *The Christian's Practice* of wearing spirituality as an all-weather garment in a spiritually stormy world. Genuine spirituality results as believers consistently work out God's design for obedience to Him.

Spiritual Maturity picks up where my last book, *Spiritual Intimacy*, left off. *Intimacy* relates to the infancy and early childhood stages of Christianity, while *maturity* addresses the developing adult Christian. Just as the Apostle John referred to little children in their intimacy (1 John 2:12-13), he also wrote to young men and fathers about spiritual maturity (2:13-14).

The author of Hebrews rejoiced that Jewish Christians had taken well to the intimacy of milk (5:12-13) but deplored their lack of advancement to the maturity of meat. So he exhorted, "Therefore leaving the elementary teaching about the Christ, let us press on to maturity" (6:1). Paul wrote with similar disappointment to the Corinthians (1 Cor. 3:1-3).

Intimacy deals fundamentally with our initial personal relationship with the Father, Son, and Holy Spirit in godwardness. Maturity, on the other hand, reflects God's abiding, growing presence in us in godliness (John 15:1-11).

Just as a baby or young child, although not yet mature, can enjoy intimacy with a parent, so should a new Christian with the freshly found Savior. But early on in the relationship, intimacy normally serves as the catalyst to initiate the maturing process, whereby a child begins to grow into parental likeness.

Intimacy without maturity results in infantile spiritual behavior instead of spiritually adult responses. In contrast, maturity without intimacy results in a stale, joyless Christianity that can easily deteriorate into legalism and sometimes even a major fall into sin.

However, Scripture teaches that when intimacy and maturity combine, a strong, vibrant Christian life pattern results. Genuine spirituality, then, cannot just be one or the other; it requires both.

The foundation for understanding spiritual maturity really begins with Scripture. Jesus, Paul, and James each directly communicated God's clear and frequent pressing demand for spiritual development in the true believer. The following passages include one or more of the key New Testament words for spiritual maturity.

Therefore you are to be perfect, *as your heavenly Father is perfect.*

Matthew 5:48

And He gave some as apostles, and some as prophets, and some as evangelists, and some as pastors and teachers, for the equipping of the saints for the work of service, to the building up of the body of Christ; until we all attain to the unity of the faith, and of the knowledge of the Son of God, to a mature *man, to the measure of the stature which belongs to the fulness of Christ.*

Ephesians 4:11-13

And we proclaim Him, admonishing every man and teaching every man with all wisdom, that we may present every man complete *in Christ.*

Colossians 1:28

All Scripture is inspired by God and profitable for teaching, for reproof, for correction, for training in righteousness; that the man of God may be adequate, *equipped for every good work.*

2 Timothy 3:16-17

Consider it all joy, my brethren, when you encounter various trials, knowing that the testing of your faith produces endurance. And let endurance have its perfect result, that you may be perfect *and* complete, *lacking in nothing.*

James 1:2-4

As you can see, prolonged infant behavior is not accepted as normal in Scripture; maturity is everywhere expected, never optional. And where maturity's expectation is matched by maturity's experience, God's commendation follows.

The quickest way to grasp the essence of maturity is to read about the obedience of people such as Abel, Noah, Abraham, Sarah, Isaac, Jacob, and Joseph in the Book of Genesis. But don't quit there. Sixty-five more books of the Bible contain additional stirring accounts of spiritual maturity. This Hall of Faith serves as the ultimate in God's affirmation of intimate faith and mature faithfulness.

Hebrews 11 chronicles spiritual maturity at its best. But notice that an exhortation immediately follows Hebrews 11 for the same kind of maturity in those who received the letter (12:1-3). It is accompanied by a warning about the Father's discipline of those who live out their Christianity immaturely (12:4-11). What's imperfectly true of earthly parenthood is but a reflection of God's flawlessly consistent response to those of us who by faith in the Lord Jesus Christ have been born again into God's family (John 1:12-13).

These crucial truths recently took on a new dimension of understanding for me when God blessed the Mayhue family with our first grandchild — Iain Michael Carson. Now I share intimate moments with him, although at ten weeks old he is incapable of maturity.

I pray that as time goes on our intimacy will ever deepen; but, more importantly, I pray that his maturity begins to develop. If it doesn't, his juvenile delinquency (spiritually speaking) will eventually erode our intimacy. It is also this way in our spiritual relationship with the Heavenly Father.

A saint of old, Epaphras, prayed that the Christians at Colossae would stand perfect and fully assured in all the will of God (Col. 4:12). May God, in similar fashion, commend these compelling biblical truths about spiritual maturity to our stewardship of worship and obedience for His own great glory. Amen!

* * * * *

If you are interested in other books on this general topic, I recommend the following:

Jerry Bridges. *The Practice of Godliness.* NavPress.

John MacArthur. *Keys to Spiritual Growth,* rev. ed. Revell.

Richard Mayhue. *Spiritual Intimacy.* Victor Books.

Kenneth Prior. *The Way of Holiness.* InterVarsity Press.

J.C. Ryle. *Holiness.* Revell.

A.W. Tozer. *The Knowledge of the Holy.* Harper and Row.

PART ONE

GOD'S PLAN

I have had a deep conviction for many years that practical holiness and entire self-consecration to God are not sufficiently attended to by modern Christians in this country. Politics or controversy or party spirit or worldliness have eaten out the heart of lively piety in too many of us. The subject of personal godliness has fallen sadly into the background. The standard of living has become painfully low in many quarters. The immense importance of "adorning the doctrine of God our Savior" (Titus 2:10), and making it lovely and beautiful by our daily habits and tempers, has been far too much overlooked. Worldly people sometimes complain with reason that "religious" persons, so-called, are not so amiable and unselfish and good-natured as others who make no profession of religion.

Yet sanctification, in its place and proportion, is quite as important as justification. Sound Protestant and Evangelical doctrine is useless if it is not accompanied by a holy life. It is worse than useless: it does positive harm. It is despised by keen-sighted and shrewd men of the world as an unreal and hollow thing, and brings religion into contempt. It is my firm impression that we want a thorough revival about Scriptural holiness, and I am deeply thankful that attention is being directed to the point.[1]

J.C. Ryle

Having therefore such a hope, we use great boldness in our speech, and are not as Moses, who used to put a veil over his face that the sons of Israel might not look intently at the end of what was fading away. But their minds were hardened; for until this very day at the reading of the old covenant the same veil remains unlifted, because it is removed in Christ. But to this day whenever Moses is read, a veil lies over their heart; but whenever a man turns to the Lord, the veil is taken away.

Now the Lord is the Spirit; and where the Spirit of the Lord is, there is liberty. But we all, with unveiled face beholding as in a mirror the glory of the Lord, are being transformed into the same image from glory to glory, just as from the Lord, the Spirit.

2 Corinthians 3:12-18

And can it be that I should gain
An interest in the Savior's blood?
Died He for me, who caused His pain?
For me, who Him to death pursued?
Amazing love! How can it be
That Thou, my God, shouldst die for me?[1]

1
THE FIRST STEP

Sportscaster Jim Nance asked America's legendary golf great, Jack Nicklaus, at a recent Master's tournament, "What has made the difference in your improved golf game?" The Golden Bear responded, "I went back to the fundamentals."

Like Nicklaus, we return to the fundamentals here before proceeding to the more advanced. Although our subject is spiritual maturity, we are first going back to spiritual infancy to outline all of the wonderful things God has done on our behalf in order for us to first understand what our salvation really involved.

Perhaps you can remember when you were saved. For me, it was on a Monday night, April 6, 1970, at Scott Memorial Baptist Church in San Diego. "B" and I struggled in our three-year-old marriage because I loved my career as a naval officer and she loved our eighteen-month-old daughter. But we had little love for each other.

Fortunately, our Christian neighbors had built a friendship with us to the point that they started inviting us to their local church. Every time we politely refused. Finally, just to appease them, I said yes to a Monday night family seminar. We figured nothing spectacular could happen on a weekday night at a Baptist church.

That evening we heard a simple Gospel presentation. I know I had heard the Gospel before, but it had never made much sense; plus, in my estimation, I really did not live badly enough to be considered a thoroughgoing sinner.

But this night proved different. Everything I heard computed. All that the preacher, Kenny Poure, said had the authority of Scripture. My sinfulness became clear in light of God's holiness—I was lost and needed to be rescued. Christ's death on my behalf and God's offer of eternal life was graciously irresistible. By the end of the service, I figured that the only logical thing to do was to accept what I so clearly needed and what God had so mercifully provided, and so I did. P.S., so did "B."

If you had asked me immediately after the service what happened, I would have reported that I heard the facts, I considered the alternatives, and I wisely chose eternal life in Christ over eternal damnation in hell. At that time, it seemed as if the whole event revolved around and depended on me.

Over the years, however, Scripture has taught me that God played the major role that night and, at best, I responded in a minor way.

In as clear and basic a way as possible, we want to review the fundamentals of salvation from God's perspective, so that we can understand what happened to us, who did what, and most importantly how salvation has changed us. We will never fully understand Christian maturity if we do not first comprehend Christian infancy!

The Rich Young Ruler

Let's first look in on a religiously oriented person who erroneously believed, as I did at one time, that salvation depended primarily on himself rather than on God. We both centered our hopes on human achievement rather than divine accomplishment.

The rich young ruler, highly interested in life beyond death, ran with urgency to publicly inquire of Jesus, "What shall I do to inherit eternal life?" (Mark 10:17) Our Lord's answer has baffled people through the centuries because He did not respond with a simple, "Believe on Me and you will have eternal life." Rather, He exposed the young man's counterfeit interest.

The inquirer betrayed his apparent sincerity by four common mistakes people make in regard to the true nature of salvation. First, he would not acknowledge his own spiritual bankruptcy by admitting that *he* could do nothing to merit eternal life (10:17). Only God could accomplish his salvation. Second, he did not acknowledge the Lord Jesus as God. He saw Him only as a good teacher who could explain the way of God (10:18). Third, he failed to recognize and repent of his own personal sinfulness (10:19-20). Rather, he extolled the self-righteous virtues of his life from his youth up. Fourth, he refused to accept the exchanged life of following the will of Christ as Savior and Lord, rather than continuing to pursue his own agenda (10:21-22).

Don't be confused here—Jesus did not teach a salvation by works. Rather, just the opposite was true. The rich young ruler tried to gain eternal life through human effort; but the Lord, through a series of questions and commands, pointed him to the real heart of true salvation extended by the mercy and grace of God. Receiving the free gift of eternal life involves at least these four elements.

- Admitting that only God can save us.
- Acknowledging Jesus Christ as God in human flesh.
- Agreeing to our personal sin which needs God's forgiveness.
- Accepting God's terms of salvation.

This encounter stands in contrast to other occasions where salvation did occur because the above truths were involved. Look at these two prime examples.

17

But the tax-gatherer, standing some distance away, was even unwilling to lift up his eyes to heaven, but was beating his breast, saying, "God, be merciful to me, the sinner!"

I tell you, this man went down to his house justified rather than the other; for every one who exalts himself shall be humbled, but he who humbles himself shall be exalted.

Luke 18:13-14

And he called for lights and rushed in and, trembling with fear, he fell down before Paul and Silas, and after he brought them out, he said, "Sirs, what must I do to be saved?" And they said, "Believe in the Lord Jesus, and you shall be saved, you and your household." . . . And he brought them into his house and set food before them, and rejoiced greatly, having believed in God with his whole household.

Acts 16:29-31, 34

The life of Paul unmistakably illustrates this point. Paul and the rich young ruler both thought identically about salvation in their youth. Before Paul met Christ, he approached salvation from a self-righteous perspective. He thought that God owed him eternal life because of who he had become and what he had done (Phil. 3:4-6).

Later, Paul recognized that he could offer nothing worthy of God, and that his best fell enormously short of meriting salvation. At that point, according to Paul's personal testimony in Philippians 3, he counted his religious past to be filthy and as repulsive as excrement. Paul then considered his whole life up to that time as a total spiritual loss in order that he might gain the things of Christ (3:7-8).

Up to that time, he had held to a form of godliness but denied its power (2 Tim. 3:5). Now, Paul turned his back on self-righteousness through human achievement, and by faith embraced Christ's righteousness through God's accomplishment. In so doing, he inherited eternal life (Phil. 3:9-11).

For confirmation of this analysis, reflect back on the historical descriptions of Paul's salvation (Acts 9:3-9; 22:6-11;

26:12-20). In the Acts 9 account, Paul acknowledged Christ's lordship and obeyed His instructions. Acts 22:10 informs us that Paul asked, "What shall I do, Lord?" Similar in verbiage to the rich young ruler but quite different in meaning, Paul actually submitted to the will of the One whom he called Lord. "I did not prove disobedient to the heavenly vision," summarizes Paul's response to God's demands (26:19).

He gave up everything of self and this life in exchange for embracing everything of God and eternal life. Although I could not have explained it at the time, that's exactly what happened to me that April evening on the corner of Oregon and Madison in San Diego. I abandoned self and fully embraced Christ.

Generation

In order to understand why human beings need to be spiritually rescued by God, let's go back to Genesis 1–2. A holy God spoke a holy world and a sinless human race into existence. At the conclusion of His six days of creation,

> *God saw all that He had made, and behold, it was very good. And there was evening and there was morning, the sixth day.*
>
> *Genesis 1:31*

Into this perfect world He placed a male and female, both created in the image of God (1:27). Although created in the image of God, they were not deity, but they shared some of the divine ability to know and think. Over this perfect world, God gave Adam and Eve dominion with the freedom to be fruitful, multiply and to fill the earth. They received only one negative command.

> *And the Lord God commanded the man, saying, "From any tree of the garden you may eat freely; but from the tree of the knowledge of good and evil you shall not eat, for in the day that you eat from it you shall surely die."*
>
> *Genesis 2:16-17*

19

Imagine a flawless world which you could enjoy forever, with only one thing that you should not do. That was the world of Adam and Eve. The human race had been "generated" by God's creative energy to enjoy God's blessing and holiness forever.

Degeneration

But the story does not end there. Satan shortly thereafter deceived Eve (2 Cor. 11:3) and both Eve and Adam violated God's prohibition (Gen. 3:1-6). As God promised, they both died.

For Adam and Eve, death involved separation. Later on their physical bodies would be separated from their spiritual beings when what we commonly think of as death occurred (Gen. 5:5). But a far more important death took place immediately after they ate—a spiritual death. At that point, their sin of disobedience separated them from unbroken communion with their holy God. The indications of this are given in Genesis 3:7-13. *results of Sun*

- Being *self* conscious— *Self-Centered*
- Hiding from God— *depression*.
- Fearing God
- Adam blaming Eve for his own actions
- Eve blaming Satan for her own actions

As a result, God cursed Satan, the woman, and Adam. Then they were evicted from the garden which housed the tree of eternal life (3:14-24).

Let's stop for a moment and put the entire Bible in perspective. Scripture can be outlined in three parts around this most important historical occurrence which resulted in God's curses.

I. Pre-curse history	Genesis 1–2
II. Curse history	Genesis 3–Revelation 20
III. Post-curse history	Revelation 21–22

Out of the 1,189 chapters in the Bible, only 4 speak of a time when the curse of Genesis 3 did not prevail. When the new heaven and new earth arrive (Rev. 21:1), there will no longer be any curse (Rev. 22:3). The remaining 1,185 chapters contrast man's utter sinfulness and inability to save himself with God's unblemished holiness, His provision in Jesus Christ for human redemption from sin and regeneration to eternal life.

As a result of Adam's sin, the entire human race has been born in sin. Although originally generated in holiness, because of Adam and Eve's fall the whole human race is now degenerate and eternally separated from God.

Behold, I was brought forth in iniquity, and in sin my mother conceived me.

Psalm 51:5

For all have sinned and fall short of the glory of God.

Romans 3:23

Scripture variously describes this spiritual death:
- Darkness of mind that needs to be enlightened by God's truth of redemption (Col. 1:13; Acts 26:18)
- Depravity of will that needs to be submitted to the orders of God (Rom. 6:11-20)
- Death of our being that needs spiritual resurrection (Eph. 2:1-7)

All of the human race needs to face the fact that we are born dead to spiritual communion with God. Thus we have but two alternatives for the future. The first is to be born again, this time into the family of God for eternal fellowship.

Now there was a man of the Pharisees, named Nicodemus, a ruler of the Jews; this man came to Him by night, and said to Him, "Rabbi, we know that You have come from God as a teacher; for no one can do these signs that You do unless God is with him."

Jesus answered and said to him, "Truly, truly, I say to you, unless one is born again, he cannot see the kingdom of God."

Nicodemus said to Him, "How can a man be born when he is old? He cannot enter a second time into his mother's womb and be born, can he?"

Jesus answered, "Truly, truly, I say to you, unless one is born of water and the Spirit, he cannot enter into the kingdom of God. That which is born of the flesh is flesh, and that which is born of the Spirit is spirit. Do not marvel that I said to you, 'You must be born again.' The wind blows where it wishes and you hear the sound of it, but do not know where it comes from and where it is going; so is everyone who is born of the Spirit."

John 3:1-8

The second alternative is to expect the second death which involves eternal separation from God in torment.

And I saw a great white throne and Him who sat upon it, from whose presence earth and heaven fled away, and no place was found for them. And I saw the dead, the great and the small, standing before the throne, and books were opened and another book was opened, which is the book of life; and the dead were judged from the things which were written in the books, according to their deeds.

And the sea gave up the dead which were in it, and death and Hades gave up the dead which were in them; and they were judged, every one of them according to their deeds. And death and Hades were thrown into the lake of fire. This is the second death, the lake of fire. And if anyone's name was not found written in the book of life, he was thrown into the lake of fire.

Revelation 20:11-15

Regeneration

With the seriousness of the second death in mind, we certainly must press on to God's salvation plan for regenerating, or generating for a second time, a holy people for eternal fellowship with Him. Degeneration demands regeneration if any human being hopes to enjoy communion with God forever.

• The Image of God. God created Adam and Eve in His image (Gen. 1:26-27; 5:1; 9:6; 1 Cor. 11:7; James 3:9). Sin has marred this glorious holy image which God in salvation renews and conforms us to the image of His Son (Rom. 8:29), by transforming us into the same image from glory to glory (2 Cor. 3:18).

Salvation not only saves us from eternal separation from God (2 Thes. 1:9-10), but it also initiates a renewal back to the original "man in the image of God" condition before the fall of Adam. Just as Christ is the image of the invisible God (Col. 1:15), so we will be changed into the likeness of Christ's perfect humanity (Col. 3:9-11).

• God's Initiative. Who is responsible for individual salvation—God or the person? Put another way, "Did God sovereignly elect us and save us? Or did He act in accord with what He knew we would do?" In other words, "Who makes the first move?"

Let me summarize what Scripture teaches about God's role in salvation. I recommend that you look up each passage so you can sense the overwhelming nature of the biblical answer.

God wills	John 1:12-13; Ephesians 1:5, 11
God draws	John 6:44
God grants	John 6:65
God calls	1 Peter 2:9; 2 Timothy 1:9
God appoints	Acts 13:48
God predestines	Romans 8:29; Ephesians 1:5, 11
God prepares	Romans 9:23
God causes	1 Corinthians 1:30
God chooses	Ephesians 1:4; 2 Thessalonians 2:13
God purposes	Ephesians 1:11
God delivers and transfers	Colossians 1:13
God saves	2 Timothy 1:9; Titus 3:5
God makes us alive	Ephesians 2:5
God pours out His Spirit	Titus 3:6
God justifies	Romans 8:30; Titus 3:7

● Man's Responsibility. Does this mean that God totally overrides the human will to impose His will? Our answer is "No!" There are other passages that teach about man's responsibility for his own sins. Think about these.

He who believes in Him is not judged; he who does not believe has been judged already, because he has not believed in the name of the only begotten Son of God.

John 3:18

It remains for some to enter it, and those who formerly had good news preached to them failed to enter because of disobedience.

Hebrews 4:6

And I saw the dead, the great and the small, standing before the throne, and books were opened; and another book was opened, which is the book of life; and the dead were judged from the things which were written in the books, according to their deeds. And the sea gave up the dead which were in it, and death and Hades gave up the dead which were in them; and they were judged, every one of them according to their deeds.

Revelation 20:12-13

People who reject the Gospel are held accountable for their sin, rather than being excused because they are the nonelect. While this is humanly impossible to completely reconcile, it nonetheless is what Scripture teaches, and so we must accept it by faith. Jesus was able to hold God's sovereignty and man's responsibility in tension without any mental reservation. Listen to Him preach the Gospel.

All things have been handed over to Me by My Father; and no one knows the Son, except the Father; nor does anyone know the Father, except the Son, and anyone to whom the Son wills to reveal Him.

Come to Me, all who are weary and heavy-laden, and I

*will give you rest. Take My yoke upon you, and learn from
Me, for I am gentle and humble in heart; and you shall
find rest for your souls. For My yoke is easy, and My load
is light.*

Matthew 11:27-30

● Christ's Death. We have redemption through Christ's
blood (Eph. 1:7) because God made peace through the blood
of His cross (Col. 1:20), in order that believers might be
reconciled to God through Christ; He did not count their
trespasses against them but rather against Christ (2 Cor.
5:18-19).

Christ's death was limited in the sense that it does not
extend to angels or animals. Nor is it redemptively applied to
all humans, but only to those who believe in the Lord Jesus
Christ according to the glorious Gospel.

On the other hand, in some senses, the atonement of
Christ was unlimited in that . . .

1. It is suitable for the whole human race.
2. It benefits all the elect in salvation.
3. Its message is extended to all in proclamation.
4. It makes common grace available to all men in noneternal ways.

These brief thoughts suggest that what was pictured as the
atonement in the Old Testament paralleled in basic ways
Christ's atonement in the New Testament. The yearly atonement in the Old (Lev. 16) anticipates Christ's once-for-all
atonement in the New (Heb. 9:1-28). It also brought common
grace to the unsaved in that God's mercy allowed them to
live yet another day rather than being immediately judged for
their sins.

● The Holy Spirit's Renewal. The work of God in salvation
vitally involves the Holy Spirit. Most Christians do not know
this, or if they do, they haven't fully realized all that this
means. Have you ever wondered why we are baptized in the
name of the Father and the Son and the Holy Spirit? (Matt.
28:19) It is symbolic identification with each member of the
Godhead in relationship to His part in our actual personal

salvation. The Spirit of God plays a significant role in salvation.

It is the Spirit who gives life; the flesh profits nothing; the words that I have spoken to you are spirit and are life.
John 6:63

But as at that time he who was born according to the flesh persecuted him who was born according to the Spirit, so it is now also.
Galatians 4:29

He saved us, not on the basis of deeds which we have done in righteousness, but according to His mercy, by the washing of the regeneration and renewing by the Holy Spirit, whom He poured out upon us richly through Jesus Christ our Savior, that being justified by His grace we might be made heirs according to the hope of eternal life.
Titus 3:5-7

The Spirit's work in salvation is sometimes called *sanctification,* in the sense of the setting apart from sin to God that takes place at salvation (1 Cor. 6:11; 2 Thes. 2:13; 1 Peter 1:2). Other terms, including "washing" and "justification," are used to show the work of God's Spirit in salvation (Rom. 8:6, 9, 23; 1 Cor. 6:11; Gal. 3:2-3, 14; 4:29; 6:8; 1 Thes. 1:5).

You might be asking how someone who is spiritually dead can be made alive? Or someone blind be made to see? Or someone overcome with evil made pure? Jesus illustrated this in the Gospels when He performed miracles of raising the dead (John 11:17-46), giving sight to the blind (John 9:1-41) and freeing people from the evil of demons (Mark 5:1-20). These miracles picture in the physical realm what occurs spiritually in salvation. Salvation begins and ends with God miraculously doing for us what we cannot do for ourselves. It is His work, not ours. It is for His glory and no one else's.

For by grace you have been saved through faith; and that

not of yourselves, it is the gift of God; not as a result of works, that no one should boast. For we are His workmanship, created in Christ Jesus for good works, which God prepared beforehand, that we should walk in them.
Ephesians 2:8-10

God has made us alive, i.e., has raised us out of being dead in sins and trespasses by the regenerating work of the Holy Spirit. As we will see shortly, what God begins with His Spirit in salvation, He continues with His Spirit in the Christian life (Phil. 1:6; Gal. 5:25). These two aspects of new life — birth and growth — always go together in Scripture.

A New Creation
True salvation is not a decision made today which will bring change only later in eternity. Regardless of how one feels or what one understands at the moment of salvation, it promises to bring with it radical change now.

Therefore if any man is in Christ, he is a new creature; the old things passed away; behold, new things have come.
2 Corinthians 5:17

Whereas I was dead, now I'm alive. Before I was blind, but now I can see. Although I was incurably stricken with sin, God has miraculously cured my transgression problem. Before I was in darkness, but today I walk in the light. Previously Satan ruled me in his domain; now I am a resident of God's kingdom. Now I am at peace with God, where before I was estranged from Him. I am a new creation (Gal. 6:15).

A saved person has laid aside the old self and has put on the new self (Col. 3:9-10). He continues to be exhorted to lay aside the former manner of life, or old self, and put on the new (Eph. 4:24). Because we are "new" in Christ:

We sing a new song (Rev. 5:9; Pss. 33:3; 40:3; 96:1; 98:1; 144:9; 149:1).

We walk in newness of life (Rom. 6:4).

We serve in newness of spirit (Rom. 7:6).

We will receive a new name (Rev. 2:17).

Put Off—Put On

As new creatures in Christ, we are clothed in Christ (Gal. 3:27) and, as a result, we are to put on Christlike behavior (Rom. 13:14). This figure of speech involves taking off the filthy rags of our old behavior and dressing our new life with the garments of righteous behavior. Here is what to put off:

Deeds of darkness	Romans 13:12
Falsehood	Ephesians 4:25
Anger	Ephesians 4:31; Colossians 3:8
Unwholesome words	Ephesians 4:29
Bitterness	Ephesians 4:31
Wrath	Ephesians 4:31; Colossians 3:8
Clamor	Ephesians 4:31
Slander	Ephesians 4:31; Colossians 3:8; 1 Peter 2:1
Malice	Colossians 3:8; 1 Peter 2:1
Abusive speech	Colossians 3:8
Lying	Colossians 3:9
Every encumbrance	Hebrews 12:1
Easily entangling sin	Hebrews 12:1
Filthiness	James 1:21
Wickedness	James 1:21
Guile	1 Peter 2:1
Hypocrisy	1 Peter 2:1
Envy	1 Peter 2:1

God doesn't want us to stand around naked, now that we have begun to shed our old lifestyle. Instead, He invites us to dress for spiritual success and provides a righteous wardrobe for our wearing (Eph. 4:24; Col. 3:10). It includes:

The armor of light	Romans 13:12
The full armor of God	Ephesians 6:11
Truth	Ephesians 4:25
Honest labor	Ephesians 4:28
Timely words of grace	Ephesians 4:29

Kindness	Ephesians 4:32; Colossians 3:12
Tenderheartedness	Ephesians 4:32
Forgiveness	Ephesians 4:32; Colossians 3:13
A heart of compassion	Colossians 3:12
Humility	Colossians 3:12
Gentleness	Colossians 3:12
Patience	Colossians 3:12
Love	Colossians 3:14
Peace of Christ	Colossians 3:15
Thankfulness	Colossians 3:15
The Word of God	Colossians 3:16
A gentle and quiet spirit	1 Peter 3:4
Submissiveness to husband	1 Peter 3:5

Reasonable Conclusions

Two great truths must be drawn before we depart the fundamentals of Christian infancy and dive headlong into "Growing in Grace." First, since God initiates and sustains our salvation, true salvation can never be forfeited. We might be short on our personal assurance, but never on the God-determined reality of our salvation.

For I am confident of this very thing, that He who began a good work in you will perfect it until the day of Christ Jesus.

Philippians 1:6

My sheep hear My voice, and I know them, and they follow Me; and I give eternal life to them, and they shall never perish; and no one shall snatch them out of My hand. My Father, who has given them to Me, is greater than all; and no one is able to snatch them out of the Father's hand.

John 10:27-29

But in all these things we overwhelmingly conquer through Him who loved us. For I am convinced that neither death, nor life, nor angels, nor principalities, nor things present, nor things to come, nor powers, nor height, nor depth, nor any other created thing, shall be able to separate us from the love of God, which is in Christ Jesus our Lord.

Romans 8:37-39

Faithful is He who calls you, and He also will bring it to pass.

1 Thessalonians 5:24

Second, since true salvation involves being raised from spiritual death and being made alive in Jesus Christ, then a true believer will show unmistakable signs of spiritual vitality and growth (James 2:14-26).

Finish then Thy new creation,
Pure and spotless let us be;
Let us see Thy great salvation
Perfectly restored in Thee.
Changed from glory into glory,
Till in heav'n we take our place,
Till we cast our crowns before Thee,
Lost in wonder, love and praise!'

2
GROWING IN GRACE

After "B" and I were saved, we discovered some wonderful new changes in our lives and marriage. Immediately, we knew that divorce would not solve our marriage problems. Rather, we needed to start all over again in order to build our home according to God's blueprint outlined in Scripture.

We also understood that our lives could no longer be lived just for ourselves; we were now servants of the God who had saved us. To the best of our remembrance, no one taught us this. It just was what we read in those fresh days of studying Scripture for the first time. We wanted to let God be God in all of our life.

Unfortunately, there are many today who believe or teach very differently about the Christian life. Listen to noted church historian, Richard Lovelace, summarize the present problem.

Like American liberalism, the modern evangelical movement has a weakened sense of the holiness of God and the depth of personal sin. The Reformation stress on justification has been retained, and also the Puritan motif of the need for regeneration. But the process of being born again is much easier than the Puritans made it: a simple immediate response of faith and commitment, often after a very short presentation of the gospel. The possibility of losing the assurance of one's salvation is not even intimated. In fact, converts are urged to believe they are saved, as though this were one of the main doctrines of the faith. The themes of holiness and continued sanctification are very much muted compared to the Puritan and awakening eras. Evangelicals are once again suffering from a sanctification gap.[2]

What Lovelace rightly diagnoses is the notion that there is no necessary or vital Christian experience after salvation and before glorification. As a result, many a Christian's life between his second birth and physical death has been seriously ignored or misunderstood by otherwise sincere Christians.

Let me illustrate what I mean with a story from the life of famous artist Michelangelo. After carefully reviewing a painting by one of his better students, the master artist wrote across the work "AMPLIUS" which in Latin means "larger."

The painting needed to be expanded—the size of the canvas enlarged. The picture, as originally done by the student, did not do justice to its grand themes and magnificent detail. A painting of worth should not be confined to such a small space that its exquisite detail could not be admired by all.

In the same manner, God would need to write "AMPLIUS" across the miniature canvas of many a Christian life. We live in a time when growth, commitment, loyalty, fervency, sacrifice, and boldness are often taught as optional Christian qualities for the elite few, when in fact God has designed every Christian to be a portrait of Christ.

I believe the biblical correction to this "sanctification gap" begins with understanding God's holy character and His holy purposes for our lives. Paul stated it this way.

So then, my beloved, just as you have always obeyed, not as in my presence only, but now much more in my absence, work out your salvation with fear and trembling; for it is God who is at work in you, both to will and to work for His good pleasure.

Philippians 2:12-13

God's Holiness

We have been saved to be holy and to live a holy life.

As obedient children, do not be conformed to the former lusts which were yours in your ignorance, but like the Holy One who called you, be holy yourselves also in all your behavior; because it is written, "You shall be holy, for I am holy."

1 Peter 1:14-16

What does it mean to be holy? Both the Hebrew and Greek words (with about 2,000 appearances in Scripture) basically mean "to be set aside for something special." In the case of God, He sets Himself apart from creation, humanity, and all pagan gods by the fact of His deity, and His sinlessness. That's why the angels sing of God, "Holy, Holy, Holy" (Isa. 6:3; Rev. 4:8).

Exalt the Lord our God, and worship at His holy hill; for holy is the Lord our God.

Psalm 99:9

I am the Lord, your Holy One, the Creator of Israel, your King.

Isaiah 43:15

Thus the idea of holiness takes on a spiritual meaning among the people of God, based on the holy character of God. For instance, the high priest of God had inscribed across his headpiece, "Holy to the Lord" (Ex. 39:30). The high priest had been especially set apart by God to intercede on behalf of a sinful nation to a holy God for the forgiveness of their transgressions.

Holiness embodies the very essence of Christianity. Our holy Savior has saved us to be a holy people (1 Peter 2:4-10). That's why one of the most common biblical names for a believer is *saint,* which simply and wonderfully means, "saved and set apart."

To all who are beloved of God in Rome, called as saints: Grace to you and peace from God our Father and the Lord Jesus Christ.

Romans 1:7

To the church of God which is at Corinth, to those who have been sanctified in Christ Jesus, saints by calling, with all who in every place call upon the name of our Lord Jesus Christ, their Lord and ours.

1 Corinthians 1:2

When we consider that a Holy God saved us, it is no surprise to learn that He gives His Holy Spirit to every believer at salvation as a gift. A primary purpose of this gift is to equip believers with the power to live a holy life.

For God has not called us for the purpose of impurity, but in sanctification. Consequently, he who rejects this is not rejecting man but the God who gives His Holy Spirit to you.

1 Thessalonians 4:7-8

And the one who keeps His commandments abides in Him, and He in him. And we know by this that He abides in us, by the Spirit which He has given us.

1 John 3:24; 4:13

So God wants us to share His holiness (Heb. 12:10) and to present ourselves as slaves of righteousness. This will result in holiness (Rom. 6:19). Listen to this challenge which contains both a negative and a positive aspect. Both are required to know holiness.

> *Therefore, having these promises, beloved, let us cleanse ourselves from all defilement of flesh and spirit, perfecting holiness in the fear of God.*
>
> *2 Corinthians 7:1*

And so it is that the author of Hebrews writes, "Make every effort to live in peace with all men and to be holy; without holiness no one will see the Lord" (12:14, NIV). Holiness is the core of a Christian's experience.

Scottish theologian John Brown boils holiness down to a definition that we can all understand and then pursue. Out of holiness springs spiritual maturity.

> *Holiness does not consist of mystic speculations, enthusiastic fervours, or uncommanded austerities; it consists in thinking as God thinks, and willing as God wills. God's mind and will are to be known from His word; and, so far as I really understand and believe God's word, God's mind becomes my mind, God's will becomes my will, and according to the measure of my faith, I become holy."*[3]

Christian Purity

Closely connected with holiness is *sanctification.* In many New Testament uses, the word seems to mean salvation (Acts 20:32; 1 Cor. 1:2). The sanctification, or being set apart in salvation, should result in our being set apart for Christian living:

> *Sanctification is an immediate work of the Spirit of God on the souls of believers, purifying their natures from the pollution and uncleanness of sin, renewing in them the image of God, and thereby enabling them, from a spiritual and habitual principle of grace, to yield obedience to God, according to the tenor of the new covenant, by virtue of the life and death of Jesus Christ. Or more briefly, it is the*

universal renovation of our natures by the Holy Spirit, into the image of God, through Jesus Christ.[4]

Sanctification includes not only the immediate act and fact of salvation, but additionally involves a progressive or growing experience of greater holiness and less sinfulness. It expresses God's will and fulfills the purpose of God's salvation call.

For this is the will of God, your sanctification; that is, that you abstain from sexual immorality; that each of you know how to possess his own vessel in sanctification and honor ... for God has not called us for the purpose of impurity, but in sanctification.

1 Thessalonians 4:3-4, 7

Sanctification includes our responsibility to participate in continuing what God's Spirit began in salvation.

Therefore, if a man cleanses himself from these things, he will be a vessel for honor, sanctified, useful to the Master, prepared for every good work.

2 Timothy 2:21

Let the one who does wrong, still do wrong; and let the one who is filthy, still be filthy; and let the one who is righteous, still practice righteousness; and let the one who is holy, still keep himself holy.

Revelation 22:11

Christians are constantly exhorted to pursue in their Christian experience what God has declared to be true of them in salvation. We are also promised that what is not now complete, God will ultimately finish in glory.

So then, my beloved, just as you have always obeyed, not as in my presence only, but now much more in my absence, work out your salvation with fear and trembling; for it is

God who is at work in you, both to will and to work for His good pleasure.

Philippians 2:12-13

Now may the God of peace Himself sanctify you entirely; and may your spirit and soul and body be preserved complete, without blame at the coming of our Lord Jesus Christ.

1 Thessalonians 5:23

This expresses one of the great paradoxes of Scripture — "We are to become what we already are and one day will be."

Whoever will call upon the name of the Lord will be saved.

Romans 10:13

For the word of the cross is to those who are perishing foolishness, but to us who are being saved it is the power of God.

1 Corinthians 1:18

And this do, knowing the time, that is already the hour for you to awaken from sleep; for now salvation is nearer to us than when we believed.

Romans 13:11

Sanctification involves the spiritual process which is pictured by a body growing into adulthood (Heb. 5:11-14) or a seed developing into a tree or flower (Ps. 1:1-6). Growth is not always easy or uniform; however, it should be the direction of a true Christian's life.

Several obstacles face the believer in this lifelong pursuit. We need to know them and be on guard to avoid or correct them as they become a part of our thinking.

- We may think more highly of ourselves than we ought and not pursue holiness as we should (Rom. 12:3).
- We may presume on salvation and assume that since we are saved, holy living is optional (Rom. 6:1-2).

- We may have been erroneously taught about the nature of Christian living and so neglect the lordship of Christ (1 Peter 3:15).
- We may be wearied by life and lack the zeal or energy to make holiness a priority (2 Cor. 7:1).
- We may think we are saved but in reality are not, then we try to live holy in the power of the flesh (Matt. 13:5-7, 20-22).

A Believer's Growth

Nature teaches us that growth is normal and to be expected; conversely, a lack of growth should sound an alarm that something is seriously wrong. So does Scripture teach, in a spiritual sense. Frequently we read in Acts that the early church grew and expanded (cf. 2:41; 4:4; 5:14; 6:7; 9:31, 35, 42; 11:21, 24; 14:1, 21; 16:5; 17:12).

We also read about God's expectations for individual growth in the Christian's life. We need to take these exhortations of Scripture seriously.

But grow in the grace and knowledge of our Lord and Savior Jesus Christ. To Him be the glory, both now and to the day of eternity. Amen.

2 Peter 3:18

Like newborn babes, long for the pure milk of the word, that by it you may grow in respect to salvation.

1 Peter 2:2

The chief agents for this growth are God's Word (John 17:17; 1 Peter 2:2) and God's Spirit (Eph. 5:15-21). When the growth occurs, we can quickly acknowledge God as the cause.

I planted, Apollos watered, but God was causing the growth. So then neither the one who plants nor the one who waters is anything, but God who causes the growth.

1 Corinthians 3:6-7

And not holding fast to the head, from whom the entire body, being supplied and held together by the joints and ligaments, grows with a growth which is from God.
Colossians 2:19

Salvation's Assurance

The Holy Spirit plays a prominent role in providing a true believer with the assurance of salvation and His assurance connects directly with growth.

The Spirit Himself bears witness with our spirit that we are children of God, and if children, heirs also, heirs of God and fellow heirs with Christ, if indeed we suffer with Him in order that we may also be glorified with Him.
Romans 8:16-17

And the one who keeps His commandments abides in Him, and He in him. And we know by this that He abides in us, by the Spirit whom He has given us.
1 John 3:24

Having formerly been spiritually dead but now made alive unto God, the believer can check his own vital signs to substantiate the fact that he is indeed alive, because he walks in the works which God has prepared (Eph. 2:1-10).

Some would teach that we only need to look at our "birth certificate" to validate new life in Christ. That is to say we need only remember the moment we put our trust in Christ and then claim the biblical promise for eternal life. They would say that how one lives after this salvation experience has little or nothing to do with validating the genuineness of one's supposed salvation.

While that is partially true, it is not biblically complete. What happens if we lose the certificate or can't remember the details of personal salvation? What if the certificate turns out to be counterfeit? The only conclusive proof is current vital signs of a spiritual nature that point to a real, continuing life.

If you want to check out your spiritual health, here are

some of the most important vital life signs of a true Christian.
Christian fruit (John 15:8).
Love for God's people (John 13:35).
Concern over personal holiness (1 Peter 1:13-21).
Love for God's Word (1 Peter 2:1-3).
Desire to obey (John 14:15, 21, 23).
Sense of intimacy with God (Rom. 8:14-17).
Perseverance (Phil. 1:27-28).
Fellowship with God's people (Heb. 10:19-25).
Desire to glorify God (Matt. 5:13-16).
Witness to Christ's reality in you (1 Peter 3:15).

Normal Christianity

*And He gave some as apostles, and some as prophets, and
some as evangelists, and some as pastors and teachers, for
the equipping of the saints for the work of service, to the
building up of the body of Christ; until we all attain to the
unity of the faith, and of the knowledge of the Son of God,
to a mature man, to the measure of the stature which
belongs to the fullness of Christ. As a result, we are no
longer to be children, tossed here and there by waves, and
carried about by every wind of doctrine, by the trickery of
men, by craftiness in deceitful scheming; but speaking the
truth in love, we are to grow up in all aspects into Him,
who is the head, even Christ, from whom the whole body,
being fitted and held together by that which every joint
supplies, according to the proper working of each individual part, causes the growth of the body for the building up
of itself in love.*

Ephesians 4:11-16

No passage in the Bible equals this paragraph in expressing
God's intention for the true believer to mature in the faith.

Three significant words are used in 4:12-13 which speak
emphatically of the normal process when God's servants her-
ald the Word of God to Christians. It is for the *equipping* of
the saints who then will do the work of ministry resulting in

the building up of the body of Christ. The goal is that each individual becomes a *mature* person.

As a result, Christians are not to linger or remain at the childhood level, but are to *grow up* in all things. As this individual maturity or growth occurs, it extends to the building up and growth of the corporate body of Christ (vv. 14-16).

Make no mistake about this process. It involves *God's Spirit* taking *God's Word* and maturing *God's people* through the ministry of *God's servants* for the *spiritual growth* of individual believers which results in the *growth of Christ's body.* God has no alternative plan for His spiritual children.

For consider Him who has endured such hostility by sinners against Himself, so that you may not grow weary and lose heart. You have not yet resisted to the point of shedding blood in your striving against sin; and you have forgotten the exhortation which is addressed to you as sons. "My son, do not regard lightly the discipline of the Lord, nor faint when you are reproved by Him; for those whom the Lord loves He disciplines, and He scourges every son whom He receives."

It is for discipline that you endure; God deals with you as with sons; for what son is there whom his father does not discipline? But if you are without discipline, of which all have become partakers, then you are illegitimate children and not sons. Furthermore, we had earthly fathers to discipline us, and we respected them; shall we not much rather be subject to the Father of spirits, and live? For they disciplined us for a short time as seemed best to them, but He disciplines us for our good, that we may share His holiness. All discipline for the moment seems not to be joyful, but sorrowful; yet to those who have been trained by it, afterwards it yields the peaceful fruit of righteousness.
Hebrews 12:3-11

IF

No better human expression of growing in grace has been written than by Amy Carmichael in her classic devotional *IF*.

It fleshes out the ultimate in Christian maturity. Enjoy this sampling and then set your heart to grow in Christ.

IF I hold on to choices of any kind, just because they are my choice; if I give any room to my private likes and dislikes, then I know nothing of Calvary love.

IF I feel injured when another lays to my charge things that I know not, forgetting that my sinless Savior trod this path to the end, then I know nothing of Calvary love.

IF there be any reserve in my giving to Him who so loved that He gave His Dearest for me; if there be a secret "but" in my prayer—"anything but that, Lord" then I know nothing of Calvary love. [5]

Immortal, invisible,
God only wise,
In light inaccessible
Hid from our eyes,
Most blessed, most glorious,
The Ancient of Days,
Almighty, victorious—
Thy great name we praise.[1]

3
WHAT IS GOD LIKE?

No more appropriate lyrics have been sung to honor the person of God than these by the four living creatures and the twenty-four elders in heaven.

Holy, Holy, Holy, is the Lord God, the Almighty, who was and who is and who is to come.

Revelation 4:8

Worthy art Thou, our Lord and our God, to receive glory and honor and power; for Thou didst create all things, and because of Thy will they existed, and were created.

Revelation 4:11

These verses describe the unblemished character of our omnipotent, sovereign God who created the universe out of nothing by a spoken word. He eternally exists before time, through time, and beyond time. Comprehending these lofty thoughts is more challenging than attempting to physically ascend Mt. Everest. God's fullness can never be fully scaled by our human minds. Writers of Scripture use the following superlatives in trying to describe God who cannot be limited or equaled.

Unsearchable	Romans 11:33
Immortal	1 Timothy 1:17
Inscrutable	Isaiah 40:28
Incorruptible	Romans 1:23
Invisible	1 Timothy 1:17
In unapproachable light	1 Timothy 6:16
Unfathomable	Romans 11:33

The Psalms abound in descriptions of God's character and works. Stop and survey this sampler in order to mentally and emotionally bask in the glorious majesty of God.

Psalm 2	Psalm 73	Psalm 139
Psalm 8	Psalm 90	Psalm 144
Psalm 18	Psalm 99	Psalm 145
Psalm 24	Psalm 104	Psalm 146
Psalm 29	Psalm 105	Psalm 147
Psalm 33	Psalm 106	Psalm 148
Psalm 50	Psalm 121	Psalm 149
Psalm 63	Psalm 135	Psalm 150

The Names of God
The names of people do not always correspond to their character or their accomplishments. But the names of God always reveal something true about Him.

● For instance, *Elohim* or God tells us that He is supreme above all things and all people (Gen. 1:1). He is eternal while all else is temporal. He is the Creator; all has been made by Him.

● *Jehovah* or Lord occurs over 6,800 times in the Old Testament and speaks of God's eternal and unchanging nature. It literally means I AM. God used it to instruct Moses (Ex.

3:13-14); and Christ confounded the Pharisees with this name (John 8:58).

• *El-Shaddai* or God Almighty points to God's invincibility and His omnipotence or all-powerfulness (Gen. 17:1-2). Nothing is too hard for God and no enemy will ever defeat Him. He can do all things.

• A fourth name is *Adonai* which means Master or Lord (Deut. 10:17). It indicates authority and ownership. Therefore, God deserves our worship, allegiance, and obedience, because from Him we have received our very existence, as well as our eternal redemption in Christ.

• Abraham unforgettably learned about *Jehovah-Jirah*, the Lord will provide, when God substituted the sacrifice to replace Isaac (Gen. 22:14). The name pictures God as seeing, and thus anticipating His divine provision of the right supply at just the right time. His omniscience or all-knowingness and wisdom are in view here.

• *Jehovah-Rophe* points to God as healer (Ex. 15:26). The Shepherd's mercy, compassion, and loving-kindness shows through this name. God's healing is to be understood both in a physical and spiritual sense.

• God's holiness can be seen in *Jehovah-M'Kaddesh* which means the Lord who sanctifies (Lev. 20:7-8). He stands as our redeemer and our sanctifier. The name reminds us that He hates sin.

• Gideon built an altar and called it *Jehovah-Shalom* (Jud. 6:24). For him it signified the quality of peace which is central to God's nature. Closely associated in a redemptive sense is *Jehovah-Tsidkenu* or Jehovah our righteousness (Jer. 23:5-6).

• *Jehovah-Rohi*, "the Lord is my Shepherd" (Ps. 23:1), and *Jehovah-Shammah*, "the Lord is there" (Ezek. 48:35), describe God's presence to guide, protect, and make provision for our needs.

The Attributes of God

An *attribute* or "characteristic quality" helps to describe the nature of something or someone. In the case of God, His attributes tell us who He is, in terms that we can understand.

Theologians categorize God's attributes in various ways; but for our purposes, we will use the descriptive phrases *noncommunicable* and *communicable*. God's noncommunicable qualities are those characteristics which are unique to deity. In contrast, communicable attributes can be reproduced, at least in part, in human beings.

● Noncommunicable Attributes. These major characteristics of God exclusively pertain to His deity. They will never be experienced by anyone else.

Omnipotence	Jeremiah 32:17
Omniscience	Psalm 139:1-6
Omnipresence	Psalm 139:7-10
Immutability	Psalm 102:27
Sovereignty	1 Chronicles 29:11-12
Eternality	Psalm 90:2
Immortality	1 Timothy 1:17
Greatness	Psalm 135:5
Self-existence	Isaiah 41:4

While we can never aspire to these qualities, they do tell us something significant about God in His relationship with us. For example, since God is all-powerful or omnipotent, nothing in life will defeat Him, and we will encounter no one or anything over which God is unable to be victorious. No problem of mine is too hard for God to solve.

Since God is omniscient, and is everywhere or omnipresent, then nothing surprises Him and He misses nothing in our lives. He will be with us in both good and bad times.

His unchangeableness or immutability, sovereignty, eternality, immortality, greatness, and self-existence all point to the exclusiveness of His deity which will be shared by no one else. Thus, we worship the one true God who is ever consistent with Himself from eternity to eternity, is dependent on nothing, will be victorious over all, and whose eternal purposes will be completely accomplished.

● Communicable Attributes. These qualities find their ultimate expression in God. However, humans can experience them to a limited degree but never in their fullest form. They include:

Wisdom	Romans 16:27
Faithfulness	1 Corinthians 10:13
Truthfulness	Exodus 34:6
Love	1 John 4:8
Goodness	Psalm 100:5
Righteousness	Psalm 92:15
Mercy	Psalm 86:15
Compassion	Lamentations 3:23
Holiness	Psalm 99:9
Graciousness	Psalm 116:5
Patience	2 Peter 3:15
Peace	Hebrews 13:20
Kindness	Psalm 100:5
Gentleness	2 Corinthians 10:1
Joy	John 17:13
Forgiveness	Exodus 34:7
Justice	Deuteronomy 10:18

At this point, you might be wondering how the attributes of God are important in our lives. Let me illustrate with a recent event at The Master's Seminary. During the recession of the early 1990s, our school needed to cut back on expenditures in order to exercise good stewardship of God's resources. It involved reducing the salaries of our professors and staff, plus raising tuition for students.

As Vice President and Dean, I had to explain this to our Seminary family. I did so in the context of God's faithfulness. I reminded them from Scripture that God is faithful (Deut. 7:9; 32:4; Pss. 36:5; 100:5). He is faithful in:

His word/promises	Hebrews 10:23
His salvation	1 Thessalonians 5:24
His protection	2 Thessalonians 3:3
His Son	Revelation 19:11
His provision	Lamentations 3:22-23

I told them that because of God's faithfulness, we had two obligations. First, we could completely trust God, even though we might not immediately see how our family budget could be balanced with a reduced salary, or how we could afford higher tuition. But as God had been faithful to accom-

47

plish His purpose in us before, so He would in the future. Therefore, we must trust Him in the same way.

Second, we could use this life opportunity to cultivate faithfulness in our own lives, families, ministries, and Seminary involvements (Prov. 12:22; 20:6). Thus we could prepare for the day when we will stand before Christ to give an account of our stewardship, when we hope we will hear the words, "Well done, thou good and faithful servant" (Matt. 25:21, 23). By understanding God's absolute dependability, trustworthiness, and reliability, we cannot only wait for His provision by faith, but also develop these same qualities in our own lives.

Close Encounters of a Spiritual Kind

Experiencing God up close often turns into a terrifying event. Whether we look at the disciples in the boat during a stormy night on the sea of Galilee (Mark 4:41), at Adam in the garden (Gen. 3:8-10), or Israel at Sinai (Ex. 20:18-21), we see a holy trauma.

● Job's Encounter. Job was blameless, upright, fearing God, and turning away from evil (Job 1:1). But when God chose to reveal Himself in a fresh way to Job, the result was fear and repentance.

You can read through the two-part oral examination that God administered to Job (38:1–40:5; 40:6–42:6). Confronted by the overwhelming noncommunicable attributes of God, Job cried out,

> *I know that Thou canst do all things, and that no purpose of Thine can be thwarted.*
>
> *Who is this that hides counsel without knowledge?*
>
> *Therefore I have declared that which I did not understand, things too wonderful for me, which I did not know.*
>
> *Hear, now, and I will speak; I will ask Thee, and do Thou instruct me.*
>
> *I have heard of Thee by the hearing of the ear; but now my eye sees Thee; therefore I retract, and I repent in dust and ashes.*
>
> *Job 42:2-6*

● Isaiah's Encounter. When this faithful prophet of God heard the seraphim sing, "Holy, Holy, Holy, is the Lord of hosts, the earth is full of His glory" (Isa. 6:3), and when he glimpsed the King's majesty, his world crumpled. Isaiah lamented,

Woe is me, for I am ruined! Because I am a man of unclean lips, and I live among a people of unclean lips; for my eyes have seen the King, the Lord of hosts.
Isaiah 6:5

Because Isaiah responded rightly over his own sin in the presence of his holy God, the Lord dispatched him on a continuing ministry of proclamation to Israel (Isa. 6:8-13). Later on God entrusted Isaiah to record some of the most moving declarations of God's attributes (Isa. 40–46). You would be greatly blessed to stop studying *Spiritual Maturity* at this point and read these great chapters by Isaiah.

● Habakkuk's Encounter. Habakkuk could not figure out why God acted as He did, in light of who he knew God to be (Hab. 1:2-4, 12-17). So on two occasions the Lord gave His prophet some postgraduate instructions on how and why God's action is always consistent with His attributes (1:5-11; 2:2-20).

The prophet's response was remarkable. First, he prayed that God would accomplish His purpose (3:1-7). Then, he recited a psalm of God's heroic deeds (3:8-15). He concluded the whole episode with these words,

I heard and my inward parts trembled; at the sound my lips quivered. Decay enters my bones, and in my place I tremble. Because I must wait quietly for the day of distress, for the people to arise who will invade us.
Habakkuk 3:16

Finally, Habakkuk promised God that regardless of what came, he would trust the Lord as his strength (3:17-19).

● Paul's Encounter. One of the really magnificent statements in Scripture about God's character was written by the Apostle Paul.

Oh, the depth of the riches both of the wisdom and knowledge of God! How unsearchable are His judgments and unfathomable His ways! For who has known the mind of the Lord, or who became His counselor? Or who has first given to Him that it might be paid back to him again? For from Him and through Him and to Him are all things. To Him be the glory forever. Amen.

Roman 11:33-36

Where did Paul learn this? I submit that this was indelibly etched in Paul's mind during his visit to the third heaven (2 Cor. 12:2). While in Paradise, he undoubtedly saw and heard things he was unable to directly communicate (2 Cor. 12:4). But Paul knew enough to believe that when God said, "My grace is sufficient for you, for power is perfected in weakness" (2 Cor. 12:9), he needed to believe and obey. So we are not surprised to read this and other wonderful expressions about God's greatness from Paul's pen.

Now to the King eternal, immortal, invisible, the only God, be honor and glory forever and ever. Amen.

1 Timothy 1:17

The Lord will deliver me from every evil deed, and will bring me safely to His heavenly kingdom; to Him be the glory forever and ever. Amen.

2 Timothy 4:18

The Ultimate Perspective

Reading about God in a book is secondhand at best. If that's all we have, so be it. But for most, if not all of us, we want to know more about God in an immediate way. Thus the Lord Jesus Christ gives us the answer.

No man has seen God at any time; the only begotten God,

who is in the bosom of the Father, He has explained Him.
John 1:18

Jesus came to explain or demonstrate God by His life. If you really want to understand the attributes of God, then carefully observe Christ in the Gospels. The attributes are all there—both noncommunicable and communicable.

Paul wrote that Christians have been predestined to become conformed to the image of the Lord Jesus Christ (Rom. 8:29). As we become like Christ, then we become like God in His communicable attributes. In so doing, the effect of the curse will be continually reversed and the image of God in man will be progressively restored.

4
TO BE LIKE GOD!

Several Christmases ago my wife introduced me to a hobby that we now dearly enjoy together—model railroading. Our "N" gauge layout represents the actual Pennsylvania Railroad on which my Grandfather Mayhue served forty years as a brakeman.

"N" gauge trains (about half the size of HO) are 1/160th the size of the real thing or prototype. As you might guess, replica models do not contain every detail of a full-size diesel engine or railcar, but no one would mistake the fact that they have been scale-modeled after the originals.

These electric trains help us to illustrate godliness. God is the prototype after whom Christians are fashioned to be scale models. We will never be identical in size to God—only miniatures; we will never possess all the characteristics of God, only those which are communicable. Put another way, we will never become or ever approach deity, but we are exhorted by Scripture to be godlike. God intends Christians to be representative copies of Himself.

Spiritual Renovation
The Bible variously describes salvation and the Christian life as going from darkness to light (Col. 1:12-13), from Satan to God (Acts 26:18), from death to life (Col. 2:13), from lust to purity (1 Peter 1:14-16), from old to new (2 Cor. 5:17), and from brokenness to being whole (Col. 2:10). Every true Christian currently experiences God's renovation or reformation. God announced the end at the beginning—we are saved. Yet He does not finish the project until the end when we are glorified. Paul described this process to the Colossians who had "put on the new self who is being renewed to a true knowledge according to the image of the One who created him" (Col. 3:10).

He told the Galatians that he labored again on their behalf until Christ be formed in them (Col. 4:19). Paul prayed that the Ephesians would be filled up with all the fullness of God (Col. 3:19). God's image in man, severely marred by sin, is made renewable by salvation so that the Christian life involves progressive restoration toward the original (Adam and Eve before the Fall) which was characterized by perfect godliness. The total perfection of godliness in a Christian will not be experienced until we are in God's presence (Phil. 1:21; 2 Cor. 5:8). Listen to Peter's explanation of salvation's effect.

Grace and peace be multiplied to you in the knowledge of God and of Jesus our Lord; seeing that His divine power has granted to us everything pertaining to life and godliness, through the true knowledge of Him who called us by His own glory and excellence. For by these He has granted to us His precious and magnificent promises, in order that by them you might become partakers of the divine nature, having escaped the corruption that is in the world by lust.
2 Peter 1:2-4

Jerry Bridges captures the essence of being godly with this insightful explanation.

> *Godliness consists of two distinct but complementary traits, and the person who wants to train himself to be godly must pursue both with equal vigor. The first trait is God-centeredness, which we call devotion to God; the second is God-likeness, which we call Christian character. Godly character flows out of devotion to God and practically confirms the reality of that devotion.*[2]

Bridges suggests that *godliness* involves first a commitment or devotion to God (God-centeredness) which then yields godlikeness in character. Both stand inseparably linked.

I would like to take his definition one more step. Mature godliness involves three, not two, elements which bloom sequentially much like a beautiful rose.
1. Godward consecration
2. Godlike character
3. Godly conduct
Now, let's see if the biblical evidence bears this out.

Biblical Godliness
The basic idea of both the Hebrew and Greek words translated "godly" centers around the general thought of devotion. The Old Testament's play on words (God's covenant lovingkindness and man's godliness) involves the concept that as God is devoted to those with whom He made a covenant, so they in turn will be devoted to Him the Covenant-Maker.

● Old Testament. Three elements of God's relationship to a godly person emerges in the Old Testament. First, God has set the godly one apart for Himself (Ps. 4:3). Second, God preserves the way of the godly (Prov. 2:8). And third, God vindicates the godly by judging the ungodly (Ps. 149:9). Interestingly, this corresponds first to the nature of salvation, then steadfastly living out the Christian life, and finally receiving eternal results.

Although the biblical information is scant, these following activities mark a godly person. Note their God-centeredness followed by both *character* and *conduct* implications.

Rejoicing in good—2 Chronicles 6:41
Singing and praising God—Psalms 30:4; 132:9, 16; 148:14
Blessing God—Psalm 145:10
Praying to God—Psalm 32:6
Loving God—Psalm 31:23

● New Testament. *Ungodliness* finds a ringing condemnation from the pen of New Testament writers.

For the wrath of God is revealed from heaven against all ungodliness and unrighteousness. . . .

Romans 1:18

But realize this, that in the last days difficult times will come. For men will be lovers of self, lovers of money, boastful, arrogant, revilers, disobedient to parents, ungrateful, unholy, unloving, irreconcilable, malicious gossips, without self-control, brutal, haters of good, treacherous, reckless, conceited, lovers of pleasure rather than lovers of God; holding to a form of godliness, although they have denied its power; and avoid such men as these.

2 Timothy 3:1-5

And about these also Enoch, in the seventh generation from Adam, prophesied, saying, "Behold, the Lord came with many thousands of His holy ones, to execute judgment upon all, and to convict all the ungodly of all their ungodly deeds which they have done in an ungodly way, and of all the harsh things which ungodly sinners have spoken against Him."

Jude 14-15

In contrast, devotion or *consecration* which marks godliness is strongly promoted by the New Testament writers.

But flee from these things, you man of God; and pursue

righteousness, godliness, faith, love, perseverance and gentleness.

1 Timothy 6:11

Now for this very reason also, applying all diligence, in your faith supply moral excellence, and in your moral excellence, knowledge; and in your knowledge, self-control, and in your self-control, perseverance, and in your perseverance, godliness; and in your godliness, brotherly kindness, and in your brotherly kindness, Christian love. For if these qualities are yours and are increasing, they render you neither useless nor unfruitful in the true knowledge of our Lord Jesus Christ. For he who lacks these qualities is blind or shortsighted, having forgotten his purification from his former sins. Therefore, brethren, be all the more diligent to make certain about His calling and choosing you; for as long as you practice these things, you will never stumble; for in this way the entrance into the eternal kingdom of our Lord and Savior Jesus Christ will be abundantly supplied to you.

2 Peter 1:5-11

We're not surprised to also see the final element—*conduct*—as a prominent feature in the New Testament discussion of godliness.

Likewise, I want women to adorn themselves with proper clothing, modestly and discreetly, not with braided hair or gold or pearls or costly garments, but rather by means of good works, as befits women making a claim to godliness.

1 Timothy 2:9-10

And indeed, all who desire to live godly in Christ Jesus will be persecuted.

2 Timothy 3:12

Since all these things are to be destroyed in this way, what sort of people ought you to be in holy conduct and godliness.

2 Peter 3:11

Paul's instruction to Titus summarizes all three aspects of godliness—consecration, character, and conduct.

For the grace of God has appeared, bringing salvation to all men, instructing us to deny ungodliness and worldly desires and to live sensibly, righteously and godly in the present age, looking for the blessed hope and the appearing of the glory of our great God and Savior, Christ Jesus; who gave Himself for us, that He might redeem us from every lawless deed and purify for Himself a people for His own possession, zealous for good deeds.

Titus 2:11-14

God's Character

In a real way, *character* sums up the Christian life. If our character conforms to the character of God through our continual consecration to or centeredness in Him, then the result will be conduct worthy of God.

You'll remember that God's character or attributes divide into two categories. His *noncommunicable* attributes are unique to His deity and found exclusively in Him. His *communicable* attributes can be formed in us by God's Spirit. God's most significant attributes which He would develop in us include:

Wisdom	Mercy	Kindness
Faithfulness	Compassion	Gentleness
Truthfulness	Holiness	Joy
Love	Graciousness	Forgiveness
Goodness	Patience	Justice
Righteousness	Peace	

Biblical godliness involves centering our focus on God whose character can be formed in us. This produces godly behavior in the true Christian. It all begins with God's grace and ultimately results in God's glory.

Godliness Illustrated

Let's take the communicable attribute of truthfulness. Everywhere Scripture declares that God is truthful. Isaiah calls

Him "the God of truth" (65:16). Titus declares that God cannot lie (1:2). The psalmist asserts that "the sum of Thy Word is truth" (119:160). God is not a man that He should lie (Num. 23:19; 1 Sam. 15:29).

Apart from God's intervention to bring salvation, man is inherently untruthful (Rom. 3:10-18). But in salvation, we turn our attentions from Satan the father of lies, and from a world full of deceit, to concentrate on God. In so doing, we begin to value truth as God values it.

Put away from you a deceitful mouth, and put devious lips far from you.

Proverbs 4:24

Two things I asked of Thee, do not refuse me before I die: Keep deception and lies far from me, give me neither poverty nor riches; feed me with the food that is my portion, lest I be full and deny Thee and say, "Who is the Lord?"

Proverbs 30:7-9

As our character conforms to God's character of truthfulness, then our lives are lived with greater truthfulness.

Therefore, laying aside falsehood, speak truth, each one of you, with his neighbor, for we are members of one another.

Ephesians 4:25

To the degree that our lives reflect truthfulness, we reflect godliness. Keep in mind, godliness is not *being* God, but rather it is bearing a likeness to God.

A Testimony of Godliness

Look for all three elements of godliness in David's wonderful expression of allegiance to God—consecration, character, and conduct. You will understand then why God called David "a man after My heart" (Acts 13:22).

And David spoke the words of this song to the Lord in the

day that the Lord delivered him from the hand of all his enemies and from the hand of Saul. And he said,

"The Lord is my rock and my fortress and my deliverer; my God, my rock, in whom I take refuge; my shield and the horn of my salvation, my stronghold and my refuge; my savior, Thou dost save me from violence. I call upon the Lord, who is worthy to be praised; and I am saved from my enemies. For the waves of death encompassed me; the torrents of destruction overwhelmed me; the cords of Sheol surrounded me; the snares of death confronted me. In my distress I called upon the Lord, yes, I cried to my God; and from His temple He heard my voice, and my cry for help came into His ears. Then the earth shook and quaked, the foundations of heaven were trembling and were shaken because He was angry. Smoke went up out of His nostrils, and fire from His mouth devoured; coals were kindled by it. He bowed the heavens also, and came down with thick darkness under His feet. And He rode on a cherub and flew; and He appeared on the wings of the wind. And He made darkness canopies around Him, a mass of waters, thick clouds of the sky. From the brightness before Him coals of fire were kindled. The Lord thundered from heaven, and the Most High uttered His voice. And He sent out arrows, and scattered them, lightning, and routed them. Then the channels of the sea appeared, the foundations of the world were laid bare, by the rebuke of the Lord, at the blast of the breath of His nostrils. He sent from on high, He took me; He drew me out of many waters. He delivered me from my strong enemy, from those who hated me, for they were too strong for me. They confronted me in the day of my calamity, but the Lord was my support. He also brought me forth into a broad place; He rescued me, because He delighted in me. The Lord has rewarded me according to my righteousness. According to the cleanness of my hands He has recompensed me. For I have kept the ways of the Lord, and have not acted wickedly against my God. For all His ordinances were before me; and as for His statutes, I did not depart from them. I was also blameless toward

*Him, and I kept myself from my iniquity. Therefore the
Lord has recompensed me according to my righteousness,
according to my cleanness before His eyes. With the kind
Thou dost show Thyself kind, with the blameless Thou dost
show Thyself blameless, with the pure Thou dost show Thyself pure, and with the perverted Thou dost show Thyself
astute. And Thou dost save an afflicted people; but thine
eyes are on the haughty whom Thou dost abase. For Thou
art my lamp, O Lord; and the Lord illumines my darkness.
For by Thee I can run upon a troop; by my God I can leap
over a wall. As for God, His way is blameless; the word of
the Lord is tested; He is a shield to all who take refuge in
Him. For who is God, besides the Lord? And who is a
rock, besides our God? God is my strong fortress; and He
sets the blameless in his way. He makes my feet like hinds'
feet, and sets me on my high places. He trains my hands
for battle, so that my arms can bend a bow of bronze. Thou
hast also given me the shield of Thy salvation, and Thy
help makes me great. Thou dost enlarge my steps under
me, and my feet have not slipped. I pursued my enemies
and destroyed them, and I did not turn back until they
were consumed. And I have devoured them and shattered
them, so that they did not rise; and they fell under my feet.
For Thou hast girded me with strength for battle; Thou
hast subdued under me those who rose up against me.
Thou hast also made my enemies turn their backs to me,
and I destroyed those who hated me. They looked, but there
was none to save; even to the Lord, but He did not answer
them. Then I pulverized them as the dust of the earth, I
crushed and stamped them as the mire of the streets. Thou
hast also delivered me from the contentions of my people;
Thou hast kept me as head of the nations; a people whom I
have not known serve me. Foreigners pretend obedience to
me; as soon as they hear, they obey me. Foreigners lose
heart, and come trembling out of their fortresses. The Lord
lives, and blessed be my rock; and exalted be God, the rock
of my salvation, the God who executes vengeance for me,
and brings down peoples under me, who also brings me out*

from my enemies; Thou dost even lift me above those who rise up against me; Thou dost rescue me from the violent man. Therefore I will give thanks to Thee, O Lord, among the nations, and I will sing praises to Thy name. He is a tower of deliverance to His king, and shows lovingkindness to His anointed, to David and his descendants forever."

2 Samuel 22:1-51

A Closing Prayer

An ancient saint captures the heart of godliness in his prayer. I commend it to us all.

> *Day by day, dear Lord,*
> *of Thee three things I pray:*
> *To see Thee more clearly*
> *To love Thee more dearly*
> *To follow Thee more nearly.*
> *(Richard of Chichester, 1197–1253)*

Breathe on me, Breath of God,
Fill me with life anew,
That I may love what Thou dost love,
And do what Thou wouldst do
Breathe on me, Breath of God,
Until my heart is pure,
Until my will is one with Thine,
To do and to endure.[1]

5
INVADED BY GOD'S SPIRIT[2]

In February 1991, I traveled to the former Soviet Union with several of my colleagues from The Master's Seminary to inaugurate a new seminary outside of Kiev in the Ukraine. While there, I taught this material on the Holy Spirit. The joy of the students in knowing the truth about His work in the believer's life still lingers prominently in my memory. I trust that your joy will be as great because you have studied Scripture about God's Holy Spirit.

Now, just as there can be no salvation without the work of the Holy Spirit (Eph. 1:13-14; Titus 3:5-6), so there can be no holy living without the ministry of the Spirit (Gal. 5:16-26; Rom. 8:1-11). The Holy Spirit is central to and indispensable in the Christian life and spiritual maturity.

Unfortunately, throughout all of church history the Spirit of God has all too often been neglected by Christians. This despite the fact that the Holy Spirit first appears in Scripture at Genesis 1:2 and is last mentioned in Revelation 22:17, with hundreds of mentions in between. Christians have frequently underrated His involvement in the kingdom plans of God.

Over the centuries some have been troubled whether or not the Holy Spirit is deity and then whether or not there really are three persons who comprise the triune Godhead. With regard to His deity, the Apostle Peter explicitly declares the Holy Spirit is God.

But Peter said, "Ananias, why has Satan filled your heart to lie to the Holy Spirit, and to keep back some of the price of the land? While it remained unsold, did it not remain your own? And after it was sold, was it not under your control? Why is it that you have conceived this deed in your heart? You have not lied to men, but to God."

Acts 5:3-4

One needs only to read a passage such as Matthew 3:16-17, which speaks of Christ being baptized, the Father pronouncing His approval from heaven, and the Holy Spirit descending on Jesus, to conclude that there are three Persons who are each Deity. That's why Jesus instructed the church to baptize in the name of the Father and of the Son and of the Holy Spirit (Matt. 28:19). Only this explanation allows for Paul's benediction to the Corinthians.

The grace of the Lord Jesus Christ, and the love of God, and the fellowship of the Holy Spirit, be with you all.

2 Corinthians 13:14

With these basic truths of the Holy Spirit's deity and triune relationship with the Son and Father affirmed, we need to examine the special truths of Scripture about the Spirit's ministry to believers in living out the Christian life. Without the Holy Spirit's continual work in a believer, there can be no true spirituality.

63

Spirit Indwelling — Presence

The Holy Spirit actively worked in Old Testament times. He was in Joshua (Num. 27:18) and Moses (Num. 11:17). The Spirit energized Samson (Jud. 13:25; 14:6, 19; 15:14). The Spirit departed from Saul (1 Sam. 16:14), and David pleaded for God not to take the Spirit from him (Ps. 51:11).

But never do we sense from Old Testament narratives that God's Spirit dwelt in every believer. In the Gospels Jesus hinted at a change that could be understood only if a new dimension of the Spirit's ministry was to begin after Christ's departure to heaven (John 14:16-17; 16:7-11). God's standard for personal holiness did not change; however, just like the progressive revelation of Scripture, there appeared to be a new level of divinely provided resource for holy living.

In the New Testament, there is explicit teaching that with the New Covenant comes a new level of divine expectation for holy living.

> *However, you are not in the flesh but in the Spirit, if indeed the Spirit of God dwells in you. But if anyone does not have the Spirit of Christ, he does not belong to Him. And if Christ is in you, though the body is dead because of sin, yet the spirit is alive because of righteousness. But if the Spirit of Him who raised Jesus from the dead dwells in you, He who raised Christ Jesus from the dead will also give life to your mortal bodies through His Spirit who indwells you.*
>
> *Romans 8:9-11*

Paul's direct statement to the fact that the Holy Spirit indwells all believers finds corroboration in other passages such as 2 Timothy 1:14 and 1 Peter 4:14.

> *Or do you not know that your body is a temple of the Holy Spirit who is in you, whom you have from God, and that you are not your own? For you have been bought with a price: therefore glorify God in your body.*
>
> *1 Corinthians 6:19-20*

As a result, the presence of God's Spirit allows Him to be:

Our source of unity	Ephesians 4:3-4
Our source of life and peace	Romans 8:6
Our source of assurance	Romans 9:1
Our source of intercession	Romans 8:26-27
Our source of instruction	1 John 2:20, 27
Our source of giftedness	1 Corinthians 12:4-11
Our source of liberty	2 Corinthians 3:18
Our source of strength	Ephesians 3:16
Our source of fruit	Galatians 5:22-23
Our source of true worship	Philippians 3:3
Our source of fellowship	Philippians 2:1
Our source of direction	Romans 8:14
Our source of ministry power	1 Corinthians 2:4

Spirit Baptism—Participation

Attendant with the Spirit's presence in our lives comes our entrance into and participation in the church universal, the body of Christ, with Spirit baptism.

> *For even with one Spirit we all were baptized into one body, whether Jews or Greeks, whether slaves or free people; and all were made to drink of one Spirit.*
> *1 Corinthians 12:13, author's translation*

This simply means that by Christ's doing Christians are immersed into the assembly of those who are saved. God has sovereignly willed this, regardless of our thoughts on the subject.

John the Baptist alerted the disciples to the forthcoming ministry of Jesus who would baptize with the Holy Spirit.

> *And John was clothed with camel's hair and wore a leather belt around his waist. . . . And he was preaching, and saying, "After me One comes who is mightier than I, and I am not even fit to stoop down and untie the thong of His sandals. I baptized you with water; but He will baptize you with the Holy Spirit."*
> *Mark 1:6-8*

65

And John bore witness saying, "I have beheld the Spirit descending as a dove out of heaven, and He remained upon Him. And I did not recognize Him, but He who sent me to baptize in water said to me, 'He upon whom you see the Spirit descending and remaining upon Him, this is the one who baptizes in the Holy Spirit.' And I have seen, and have borne witness that this is the Son of God."

John 1:32-34

Jesus testified to the same truth just before He ascended into heaven.

And gathering them together, He commanded them not to leave Jerusalem, but to wait for what the Father had promised, "Which," He said, "you heard of from Me; for John baptized with water, but you shall be baptized with the Holy Spirit not many days from now."

Acts 1:4-5

When Cornelius, the Gentile centurion, was saved along with his household, Peter remembered this promise and used it to explain how he knew salvation had come to those people.

"And as I began to speak, the Holy Spirit fell upon them, just as He did upon us at the beginning. And I remembered the word of the Lord, how He used to say, 'John baptized with water, but you shall be baptized with the Holy Spirit.' If God therefore gave to them the same gift as He gave to us also after believing in the Lord Jesus Christ, who was I that I could stand in God's way?" And when they heard this, they quieted down, and glorified God, saying, "Well then, God has granted to the Gentiles also the repentance that leads to life."

Acts 11:15-18

We need to understand several features about Jesus baptizing us with the Holy Spirit.

- Spirit baptism is inseparably linked with salvation.
- Spirit baptism, like salvation, occurs only once.
- In Spirit baptism, Christ does the baptizing and the Holy Spirit is the medium into which we are immersed.
- The isolated historical instances where tongues speaking was accompanied with Spirit baptism were associated with the apostolic era and are not normal for today (Acts 2:4; 10:46; 19:6).
- God initiates Spirit baptism; we do not have to seek it.
- Spirit baptism is the means by which God places us in His church (1 Cor. 12:13).

Spirit Sealing—Promise

Just as a young man gives a young lady an engagement ring to validate his promise to marry her, so God gives every believer the Holy Spirit as a down payment. This assures us of His promise to complete what He began with regard to our marriage to Christ resulting in eternal life.

Now He who establishes us with you in Christ and anointed us is God, who also sealed us and gave us the Spirit in our hearts as a pledge.

2 Corinthians 1:21-22

Now He who prepared us for this very purpose is God, who gave to us the Spirit as a pledge.

2 Corinthians 5:5

In Him, you also, after listening to the message of truth, the gospel of your salvation—having also believed, you were sealed in Him with the Holy Spirit of promise, who is given as a pledge of our inheritance, with a view to the redemption of God's own possession, to the praise of His glory.

Ephesians 1:13-14

And do not grieve the Holy Spirit of God, by whom you were sealed for the day of redemption.

Ephesians 4:30

These passages on the sealing of our souls by God with the Holy Spirit leads us to several conclusions.

- We are never commanded or told to seek sealing.
- God sovereignly seals us with the Holy Spirit as a part of our salvation.
- Sealing identifies us as an everlasting possession of God.
- Sealing promises God's protection against spiritual enemies.
- Sealing guarantees our ultimate redemption by God who saved and sealed us for the purpose of eternal life.
- Sealing is to the praise of God's glory.

Spirit Fruit — Production
The clearest passage on this wonderful ministry of the Holy Spirit occurs in Galatians 5:13-26.

For you were called to freedom, brethren; only do not turn your freedom into an opportunity for the flesh, but through love serve one another. For the whole Law is fulfilled in one word, in the statement, "You shall love your neighbor as yourself." But if you bite and devour one another, take care lest you be consumed by one another.

But I say, walk by the Spirit, and you will not carry out the desire of the flesh. For the flesh sets its desire against the Spirit, and the Spirit against the flesh; for these are in opposition to one another, so that you may not do the things that you please. But if you are led by the Spirit, you are not under the Law.

Now the deeds of the flesh are evident, which are: immorality, impurity, sensuality, idolatry, sorcery, enmities, strife, jealousy, outbursts of anger, disputes, dissensions, factions, envyings, drunkenness, carousings, and things like these, of which I forewarn you just as I have forewarned you that those who practice such things shall not inherit the kingdom of God.

But the fruit of the Spirit is love, joy, peace, patience, kindness, goodness, faithfulness, gentleness, self-control; against such things there is no law. Now those who belong to Christ Jesus have crucified the flesh with its passions and desires. If we live by the Spirit, let us also walk by the Spirit. Let us not become boastful, challenging one another, envying one another.

Paul contrasted the deeds of the flesh, carnality, with the fruit of the Spirit, spirituality. He insisted that the believer must walk by the Spirit (vv. 16, 25), and be led by the Spirit (v. 18). Several chapters earlier, he had challenged the Galatians.

This is the only thing I want to find out from you: did you receive the Spirit by the works of the Law, or by hearing with faith? Are you so foolish? Having begun by the Spirit, are you now being perfected by the flesh?
Galatians 3:2-3

At times they, like we, wanted to return to the works of the law and the deeds of the flesh. To do this, however, would be to give up their freedom in salvation and be enslaved once more to sin.

Note carefully that the flesh and the Spirit stand in direct opposition to one another (5:17). Because of this contrast, to walk by the Spirit is to avoid walking in the flesh. When we start to walk in the flesh, the warning signs are evident (5:19). They do not correspond to kingdom behavior (5:21).

In *Spiritual Intimacy* I defined each element in the fruit of the Spirit from the Greek text. The definitions are personalized in action form. I encourage you to review that material, on page 102, before going on.

Now, let me take us a step further and compare the fruit of the Spirit with the character of God and then with His commands that we live out His character in our lives.

● The Character of God.

Love	God is love (1 John 4:16)
Joy	The town of My joy (Jer. 49:25)
Peace	The God of peace (Heb. 13:20)
Patience	God is patient with us (2 Peter 3:9)

Kindness   God's kindness to us (Eph. 2:7)
Goodness   The goodness of the Lord (Ps. 27:13)
Faithfulness   God is faithful (1 Cor. 10:13)
Gentleness   Christ is gentle and humble in heart
                 (Matt. 11:29)
Self-control   The divine nature includes self-control
                 (2 Peter 1:4, 6)

● The Commands of Scripture.

Love   You shall love (Matt. 22:37, 39)
Joy   Rejoice in the Lord (Phil. 4:4)
Peace   Seek peace and pursue it (1 Peter 3:11)
Patience   Be patient with all men (1 Thes. 5:14)
Kindness   Put on ... kindness (Col. 3:12)
Goodness   Let us do good to all men (Gal. 6:10)
Faithfulness   Be faithful until death (Rev. 2:10)
Gentleness   Make a defense ... with gentleness
                 (1 Peter 3:15)
Self-control   Add to your knowledge self-control
                 (2 Peter 1:6)

Spirit Giftedness—Provision

Countless volumes have been written on spiritual gifts. But in short order, I want to outline the basics with four questions and the appropriate biblical answers.

● What Do I Need to Know about Spiritual Gifts?

1. Salvation is a "charisma" or free gift (Rom. 6:23).
2. God's Holy Spirit is a gift as a part of salvation (Rom. 5:5; 1 Thes. 4:8; 1 John 3:24; 4:13).
3. Every believer has received a spiritual gift—spiritual in source and nature (1 Peter 4:10; 1 Cor. 1:7; 7:7).
4. God's will, not man's, is the criterion for who gets what gift (1 Cor. 12:11, 18).
5. Spiritual gifts are diverse (1 Cor. 12:12-27). Of the several gift lists in the New Testament, no two are the same (Rom. 12:6-8; 1 Cor. 7:7-8; 12:8-10; 12:28-30; 13:1-3, 8).
6. In the qualities desired for church leaders and mature believers, spiritual gifts are never mentioned (1 Cor.

13:4-7; Gal. 5:22-23; 1 Tim. 3:1-7; Titus 1:5-9).

7. The kind of spiritual gifts people are given do not necessarily indicate their level of spirituality.

● How Can I Identify My Spiritual Gift?

1. Believing that God has uniquely gifted you, the focus should be more on gift than gifts (1 Peter 4:10).
2. Your spiritual gift will come as a result of salvation.
3. You will be able to maximize ministry with minimum effort.
4. Sooner or later, others will recognize and comment on your spiritual gift.
5. Your spiritual gift will be used most effectively in the context of the local church.
6. If you can't identify your spiritual gift, still get involved.
7. Your inclinations and the observations of others will lead you to fruitful ministry.

● What Should I Do with My Spiritual Gift?

1. Build up the church (1 Cor. 14:12).
2. Serve one another (1 Cor. 12:7; 1 Peter 4:10).

● What Errors Should I Avoid in Exercising My Spiritual Gift?

1. Self-edification rather than the orientation of others (1 Peter 4:10).
2. Self-exercise rather than being Spirit-exercised (1 Peter 4:11).
3. Self-exaltation rather than for God's glory (1 Peter 4:11).

Spirit Filling—Power

The concept of filling does not *first* appear in the New Testament, but rather in Exodus 31:3 and 35:31 when it refers to a special enablement of Bezalel by God to craft the tabernacle. And in Luke 1, before the birth of Jesus, we discover the spirit-filled family: Zacharias (1:67), Elizabeth (1:41), and John the Baptist while yet in the womb (1:15).

Most instructive is that which was said about Christ.

And Jesus, full of the Holy Spirit, returned from the Jordan and was led about by the Spirit in the wilderness.

Luke 4:1

Jesus was totally controlled by God's Spirit, which is the basic idea of "full of the Holy Spirit." Therefore, *He was led about by the Spirit.* Simply put, Christ totally submitted to the leadership of the Spirit and was perfectly obedient to the Spirit's direction in His wilderness experience. Please do not make this wonderful truth difficult or complex. What Christ lived out in His humanity, we also are to live out in our Christian experience.

You might ask, "Why should I be filled with the Spirit?" We are never commanded to be baptized, indwelt, sealed, or gifted by the Spirit. But we are commanded to be *filled.*

Therefore be careful how you walk, not as unwise men, but as wise, making the most of your time, because the days are evil. So then do not be foolish, but understand what the will of the Lord is.

And do not get drunk with wine, for that is dissipation, but be filled with the Spirit, *speaking to one another in psalms and hymns and spiritual songs, singing and making melody with your heart to the Lord; always giving thanks for all things in the name of our Lord Jesus Christ to God, even the Father; and be subject to one another in the fear of Christ.*

Ephesians 5:15-21

To best understand how spiritual filling works, I want to conclude by quoting a section from *Spiritual Intimacy* (pp. 116–17).

God's will involves God's Spirit literally controlling our lives and giving us spiritual direction. How does He do this and how can we cooperate in this spiritual venture? Look at Colossians 3:16-17, and you'll discover that letting the Word of God dwell in you richly produces the same spiritual qualities as letting God's Spirit control you. The simple but profound conclusion is that God's Word energizes man's mind to obey God's Spirit.

If we do this, what will it produce? First, godly conversation (Eph. 5:19). We will communicate heavenward with songs of praise to God and horizontally to each other with words of spiritual joy. Second, a thankful reaction to all of life (5:20). Third, a submitted relationship to one another in the fellowship of Christ that will extend from our marriage and family life (5:22–6:4) into the work world (6:5-9) and beyond (6:10-20).

This answers the "how" and "what" raised by Peter's exhortation "to live the rest of the time in the flesh no longer for the lusts of men, but for the will of God" (1 Peter 4:2). We fuel the process by taking megadoses of God's Word. We check our progress by looking at three areas of life: (1) our rhetoric, (2) our reactions, and (3) our relationships. If you need a mentor in these areas, let Barnabas be your model (Acts 11:22-24).

Holy Bible, Book divine
Precious treasure, thou art mine;
Mine to tell me whence I came;
Mine to teach me what I am.
Mine to chide me when I rove;
Mine to show a Savior's love.
Mine thou art to guide and guard;
Mine to punish or reward.[1]

6
IMPACTED BY GOD'S WORD

Let's start this chapter with an "agree/disagree" question. "When it comes to spiritual matters, all we need to know is revealed in God's Word and ministered to us by His Spirit."[2]

Think twice about the statement before you finalize your answer. Where you stand on this ultimately decides where you land on every spiritual issue. What do you think the Apostle Paul would say? Undoubtedly, he would tell us what he said to Timothy.

> *All Scripture is inspired by God and profitable for teaching, for reproof, for correction, for training in righteousness; that the man of God may be adequate, equipped for every good work.*
>
> 2 Timothy 3:16-17

And what about King David?

The law of the Lord is perfect, restoring the soul; the testimony of the Lord is sure, making wise the simple. The precepts of the Lord are right, rejoicing the heart; the commandment of the Lord is pure, enlightening the eyes.

The fear of the Lord is clean, enduring forever; the judgments of the Lord are true; they are righteous altogether. They are more desirable than gold, yes, than much fine gold; sweeter also than honey and the drippings of the honeycomb. Moreover, by them Thy servant is warned; in keeping them there is great reward.

Psalm 19:7-11

Both David and Paul would uncompromisingly answer, "Agree!" On the other hand, what would the implication be if someone disagreed? To answer that, let's look in on a group of people who did answer that way and hear what the Lord Jesus Christ thought of their response.

When Jesus received the Pharisees' rebuke that His disciples did not wash according to Jewish tradition, He confronted them with the consequences of rejecting the all-sufficiency of God's Word and relying on a mixture of man's religious traditions and God's truth.

Christ indicted the Pharisees on two counts. First, He accused them, "Neglecting the commandment of God, you hold to the tradition of men" (Mark 7:8).

Second, He said they had *rejected* God's Word (7:9-12). "You nicely set aside the commandment of God in order to keep your tradition" (v. 9). Jesus concluded that to both neglect and reject, which is to say Scripture alone is not sufficient in spiritual matters, results in negating the validity of Scripture (7:13).

If Scripture can be neglected and/or rejected in whole or in part, then there is no significance in a claim like Paul's or David's as to the completeness of the Bible. Therefore to disagree with our beginning question is to disagree not with John MacArthur, but with Scripture itself. If you disagreed, you will be at odds with God who testified,

Every word of God is flawless; He is a shield to those who take refuge in Him. Do not add to His words, or He will rebuke you and prove you a liar.

Proverbs 30:5-6 (NIV)

Loving God's Word

The psalmists would wholeheartedly agree that Scripture is sufficient. We want to listen in on the heart and mind of a spiritually mature approach to the Bible found in the longest Psalm (176 verses) and the most complete text speaking about the whole of Scripture.

The author of Psalm 119 does not identify himself, although through the years David, Ezra, or Daniel have been suggested by godly scholars. In this study, we want to note the features of a person who has been impacted by God's Word. These qualities characterize mature Christianity as evidenced by one's response to Scripture.[3]

The psalmist craved God's Word with an insatiable appetite. He understood that his spiritual vitality depended on an abundant intake of Scripture. These phrases from Psalm 119 stress the ultimate importance of God's Word to this believer.

Loves the Word	119:47-48, 97, 113, 127, 140, 159, 163, 165, 167
Delights in the Word	119:16, 24, 35, 47, 70, 77, 92, 143, 174
Longs for the Word	119:19-20, 40, 131
Waits for the Word	119:38, 43
Finds joy in the Word	119:111, 162
Esteems the Word	119:128
Stands in awe of the Word	119:161

The psalmist responded to the Word like the Thessalonians to whom Paul wrote,

And for this reason we also constantly thank God that when you received from us the word of God's message, you

accepted it not as the word of men, but for what it really is, the word of God, which also performs its work in you who believe.

1 Thessalonians 2:13

Hating Sin

His love for God's Word resulted in a predictable corollary—he hated sin because God hates sin. A constant reading about God who is holy will give us the same attitude toward sin as we see in God.

The psalmist spoke against:

The arrogant	119:21-22
The wicked	119:53
The false way	119:104
The double-minded	119:113
The evildoers	119:115
The deceitful	119:118
The lawbreakers	119:126

Of all the characteristics of God that he mentions, one stands out far more frequently than others—the covenant loving-kindness of God to forgive those who repent of their sins and turn to God in faith for salvation (Ps. 119:41, 64, 76, 88, 124, 149, 159). When referring to the nature of God's Word, the psalmist most often focuses on a corollary to God's covenant kindness—the righteousness of God's Word which reflects God's just character (Ps. 119:7, 62, 106, 123, 144, 160, 164, 172).

The psalmist so detests sin that he confesses, "My eyes shed streams of water, because they do not keep Thy law" (119:136). In a positive response to the presence of sin, he asks a key question and then answers like this,

How can a young man keep his way pure? By keeping it according to Thy word. With all my heart I have sought Thee; do not let me wander from Thy commandments. Thy word I have treasured in my heart, that I may not sin against Thee.

Psalm 119:9-11

Questing to Know God's Mind

The writer so deeply desired to understand God's Word that on at least seven occasions he cried for God to give him understanding (Ps. 119:27, 34, 73, 100, 125, 144, 169), and prayerfully invited God to be his teacher (119:12, 26, 33, 64, 66, 68, 108, 124, 135). Listen to the resulting testimony.

> *I have not turned aside from Thine ordinances, for Thou Thyself hast taught me.*
>
> *Psalm 119:102*

The psalmist knew that he was dependent upon God for light (119:105), sight (119:18), insight (119:99), and wisdom (119:98). This became so important to him that he promised God that he would not forget God's Word (119:16, 93, 176). He put a premium on possessing Scripture for immediate recall; he unquestionably memorized Scripture for this to become reality.

God's ministry of illumination by which He gives us light on the meaning of Scripture (119:130) is in view here. Paul and John affirm this also in the New Testament.

> *I pray that the eyes of your heart may be enlightened, so that you may know what is the hope of His calling, what are the riches of the glory of His inheritance in the saints, and what is the surpassing greatness of His power toward us who believe. These are in accordance with the working of the strength of His might.*
>
> *Ephesians 1:18-19*

> *And as for you, the anointing which you received from Him abides in you, and you have no need for anyone to teach you; but as His anointing teaches you about all things, and is true and is not a lie, and just as it has taught you, you abide in Him.*
>
> *1 John 2:27*

The truth about God illuminating Scripture should greatly

encourage us. While it does not eliminate the need for gifted men to teach us (Eph. 4:11-12; 2 Tim. 4:2), or the hard labor of serious Bible study (2 Tim. 2:15), it does promise that we do not need to be enslaved to church dogma or be led astray by false teachers. Our primary dependence for learning Scripture needs to be upon the Author of Scripture—God Himself. Thus we can be like the Bereans who compared every teaching of man with God's Word to determine if man's words were true or not (Acts 17:11).

Meditating on God's Word
This spiritual man made Scripture his constant mental companion. He thrived on contemplating or thinking about God's Word (119:15, 23, 27, 48, 78, 97, 99, 148). His mind-set became more like God's through constant exposure and repetition. He purified his thinking by continually washing it in the pure water of God's Word. Because he thought like God, then he could progressively live according to God's will as outlined in His Word (Prov. 23:7). Here is a good way to determine your success with meditation.

We can test ourselves by asking whether our spiritual thoughts are like guests visiting a hotel, or like children living at home. There is a temporary stir and bustle when guests arrive, yet within a little while they leave and are forgotten. The hotel is then prepared for other guests. So it is with religious thoughts that are only occasional. But children belong to their house. They are missed if they don't come home. Preparation is continually being made for their food and comfort. Spiritual thoughts that arise from true spiritual mindedness are like the children of the house—always expected, and certainly enquired for if missing. [4]

Finding Comfort/Counsel in God's Truth
The psalmist did not live or minister in the best of circumstances (119:81-88, 145-152). Yet, he looked to God for comfort in the midst of affliction (119:49-50, 52, 76-77, 82, 84-86).

He also sought counsel (119:24) which gave him more insight than all his teachers, more wisdom than his enemies, and greater understanding than the aged (119:98-100).

It's no wonder that the Word encouraged him in tough times or gave him greater understanding than others. Listen to how the psalmist describes some of the qualities of Scripture which parallel the attributes of God.

Good	119:39
True	119:43, 142, 151, 160
Trustworthy	119:42
Faithful	119:86
Light	119:105
Pure	119:140
Eternal	119:89, 152
Unchangeable	119:89

Combining Prayer with God's Word

It is difficult in Psalm 119 to distinguish at times where testimony ends and prayer begins. The psalm resembles a two-way conversation, although we hear only the psalmist. However, we know that he has heard God in His Word and now responds in a most personal and verbal way. Listen to a few examples of his requests.

Oh that my ways may be established to keep Thy statutes!
Psalm 119:5

Remove the false way from me and graciously grant me Thy law.
Psalm 119:29

Incline my heart to Thy testimonies, and not to dishonest gain.
Psalm 119:36

I entreated Thy favor with all my heart;
be gracious to me according to Thy Word.
Psalm 119:58

Establish my footsteps in Thy Word, and do not let any iniquity have dominion over me.

Psalm 119:133

Walking Obediently
Christians must be strongly confronted with the need for obedience. Paul found it necessary to so rebuke the Corinthians.

And I, brethren, could not speak to you as to spiritual men, but as to men of flesh, as to babes in Christ. I gave you milk to drink, not solid food; for you were not yet able to receive it. Indeed, even now you are not yet able, for you are still fleshly. For since there is jealousy and strife among you, are you not fleshly, and are you not walking like mere men?

1 Corinthians 3:1-3

They did not have the same constant companionship of the Scripture as did the psalmist. He passionately desired to walk obediently to God's commandments (Ps. 119:4, 8, 30-32, 44-45, 51, 55, 59-61, 67-68, 74, 83, 87, 101-102, 110, 112, 141, 157). Take note of his constant promises to God.

The Lord is my portion; I have promised to keep Thy words.

Psalm 119:57

I am a companion of all those who fear Thee, and of those who keep Thy precepts.

Psalm 119:63

I have sworn, and I will confirm it, that I will keep Thy righteous ordinances.

Psalm 119:106

Thy testimonies are wonderful; therefore my soul observes them.

Psalm 119:129

My soul keeps Thy testimonies, and I love them exceedingly. I keep Thy precepts and Thy testimonies, for all my ways are before Thee.

Psalm 119:167-168

Praising God Continually

Praise permeates Psalm 119. The psalmist sings (119:54, 172), gives thanks (119:7, 62, 108), and rejoices (119:13-14). His gratefulness abounds (119:65, 151-152, 160).

He testifies that seven times daily the praise of God breaks forth from his lips over the righteous ordinances of the law (119:164). He even prays that God will sustain his praise.

Let my lips utter praise, for Thou dost teach me Thy statutes.

Psalm 119:171

Let my soul live that it may praise Thee, and let Thine ordinances help me.

Psalm 119:175

When we consider the richness of God's Word, we're not surprised at the psalmist's praise. In Psalm 119, eight different terms are used to describe God's Word—each indicating a particular characteristic or function.[5]

Law	119:1
Word	119:9
Judgments	119:7
Testimonies	119:2
Commands	119:6
Statutes/decrees	119:5
Precepts	119:4
Word/promise	119:11

Valuing Scripture Highly

According to the psalmist (119:72, 127), Scripture has greater value than money. It brings more pleasure than the sweetness of honey (119:103). Maturity (119:3) and blessing (119:1-

2) are the results of obedience to it. No wonder he exalted Scripture so highly—just as did the writers of Proverbs.

The one who despises the Word will be in debt to it, but the one who fears the commandment will be rewarded.
Proverbs 13:13

He who gives attention to the Word shall find good, and blessed is he who trusts in the Lord.
Proverbs 16:20

He who keeps the commandment keeps his soul, but he who is careless of his ways will die.
Proverbs 19:16

Appealing to God for Deliverance

The promise of Scripture gave the psalmist courage to squarely face life's trials (119:46, 75, 89-91, 116-117). He believed that a righteous testing would come from keeping God's Word (119:80) and personal peace with God would be his (119:165).

One of the most constant pleas throughout Psalm 119 is for *revival*. The psalmist needed revival in the sense that life and his enemies had worn him down; so he appealed to God for renewed physical, emotional, and spiritual vitality (119:25, 37, 40, 50, 88, 93, 107, 149, 154, 156, 159).

Even more frequent than his prayer for revival is a repeated plea for deliverance. Sometimes it is not clear whether he speaks of rescue from his human enemies or salvation from sin and its damnable consequences. The latter, in its ultimate sense, would provide the former, in its final sense (119:41-42, 81, 94, 109, 123, 134, 146, 153-154, 166).

Where did he get his courage? Certainly, it came from being saturated with a knowledge of God's character as taught in Scripture. Notice this sample of references to God in Psalm 119.

| God's goodness | 119:68 |
| God's creatorship | 119:73, 90 |

God's judgment   119:75, 84, 120, 137
God's faithfulness   119:75, 90
God's compassion   119:77
God's righteousness   119:137, 142
God's mercy   119:156

To close the psalm, he prays for the blessing that he wrote about in the first two verses.

Let Thy hand be ready to help me, for I have chosen Thy precepts. I long for Thy salvation, O Lord, and Thy law is my delight. Let my soul live that it may praise Thee, and let Thine ordinances help me. I have gone astray like a lost sheep; seek Thy servant, for I do not forget Thy commandments.

Psalm 119:173-176

Becoming a Psalm 119 Person

Understandably, you might be a little overwhelmed by now — but that's unnecessary. Augustine supposedly commented on Psalm 119 in this fashion, "It seems not to need an expositor, but only a reader and listener." His point is that anyone who is serious about God's Word can understand this psalm and apply its principles to life. It's not just for scholars; rather God intended it for anyone who takes Scripture seriously.

One personal characteristic of the psalmist stands out noticeably. From sunrise to beyond sunset, the Word of God dominated his life.

At dawn   119:147
Daily   119:97
Seven times daily   119:164
Nightly   119:55, 148
At midnight   119:62

Three simple habits can give you what the psalmist experienced.

1. Read in God's Word every day of your life.[6]
2. Think in God's Word frequently.
3. Walk in God's Word continuously.

This free-verse poem captures the spirit of our psalmist; I hope it captures your spirit also.

New Bible

This was an exciting day for me, Lord!
This morning I opened my new Bible.
Not a single word was circled,
Not a single phrase underlined.
Now with each new day
I can circle and underline again.
I can word-clutter the margins.
And I know what will happen, Lord—
I'll be asking as I read
Why didn't I see that before?
But even with the joy of a new Bible,
I'm going to miss my old one
With its tattered pages—
Its creased and torn edges.
Oh, how many personal notes
Are jotted on the margins!
How many God-whispered secrets!
Yes, Lord, I'll miss it.
But thank you for a friend's reminder:
"If your Bible is falling apart
Chances are your life isn't."[7]

Oh to be like Thee! blessed Redeemer,
This is my constant longing and prayer;
Gladly I'll forfeit all of earth's treasures,
Jesus, Thy perfect likeness to wear.[1]

7
SPIRITUAL TRANSFORMATION

Being a former naval officer, I was delighted one day to find *A Sailor's Dictionary* while browsing through my favorite bookstore. The dust jacket read, "A dictionary for landlubbers, old salts and armchair drifters." It sounded inviting.

Intrigued, I picked up the book to sample the humor. Here's how it described *sailing*—"The fine art of getting wet and becoming ill while slowly going nowhere at great expense."[2] I thought, "That's true not only of sailing but also of the spiritual life, unless we are directed by the gentle breeze of God's transforming wisdom."

Wisdom's Source

Wisdom shouts in the street, she lifts her voice in the square; at the head of the noisy streets she cries out; at the

*entrance of the gates in the city, she utters her sayings:
"How long, O naive ones, will you love simplicity? And
scoffers delight themselves in scoffing, and fools hate
knowledge? Turn to my reproof, behold, I will pour out my
spirit on you; I will make my words known to you. Because
I called, and you refused, I stretched out my hand, and no
one paid attention; and you neglected all my counsel, and
did not want my reproof; I will even laugh at your calamity; I will mock when your dread comes, when your dread
comes like a storm, and your calamity comes on like a
whirlwind, when distress and anguish come on you.*

*"Then they will call on me, but I will not answer; they
will seek me diligently, but they shall not find me, because
they hated knowledge, and did not choose the fear of the
Lord. They would not accept my counsel, they spurned all
my reproof. So they shall eat of the fruit of their own way,
and be satiated with their own devices. For the wayward-
ness of the naive shall kill them, and the complacency of
fools shall destroy them. But he who listens to me shall live
securely, and shall be at ease from the dread of evil."*

Proverbs 1:20-33

The writer of Proverbs puts wisdom in street language.
Portrayed as a woman crying out in the city, wisdom beckons
the people to turn from their sinful scoffing to the reproof of
God and its attendant reward (vv. 23, 33).

Jesus parallels this same idea with His Parable of the Two
Builders.

*Therefore everyone who hears these words of Mine, and
acts upon them, may be compared to a wise man, who built
his house upon the rock. And the rain descended, and the
floods came, and the winds blew, and burst against that
house; and yet it did not fall, for it had been founded upon
the rock.*

*And everyone who hears these words of Mine, and does
not act upon them, will be like a foolish man, who built his
house upon the sand. And the rain descended, and the*

floods came, and the winds blew, and burst against that house; and it fell, and great was its fall.
Matthew 7:24-27

Our spiritual transformation begins when we receive Jesus Christ as Savior and Lord. Paul describes Him as the one "in whom are hidden all the treasures of wisdom and knowledge" (Col. 2:3; see 1 Cor. 1:24, 30). The Spirit of God comes to indwell us with what Isaiah calls, "The spirit of wisdom and understanding, the spirit of counsel and strength, the spirit of knowledge and the fear of the LORD" (Isa. 11:2). Paul reminds us that the one to whom glory will be given forever is "the only wise God" (Rom. 16:27) referring to God the Father. Our relationship to Father, Son, and Holy Spirit refers to a union with pure wisdom. Thus we are transformed by the personal presence and power of wisdom in our lives.

Wisdom's Manner
God's will, His Word, and His way are all wise. Everything about God is wise; all else is foolishness. This little catechism answers several key questions about wisdom from Scripture.
● Place—Where Can Wisdom Be Found?

The law of the Lord is perfect, restoring the soul; the testimony of the Lord is sure, making wise the simple.
Psalm 19:7

You, however, continue in the things you have learned and become convinced of, knowing from whom you have learned them; and that from childhood you have known the sacred writings which are able to give you the wisdom that leads to salvation through faith which is in Christ Jesus.
2 Timothy 3:14-15

● Pattern—What Identifies True Wisdom?

The fear of the Lord is the beginning of wisdom, and the knowledge of the Holy One is understanding.
Proverbs 9:10

● Profit—How Valuable Is Wisdom?

How blessed is the man who finds wisdom, and the man who gains understanding. For its profit is better than the profit of silver, and its gain than fine gold. She is more precious than jewels; and nothing you desire compares with her. Long life is in her right hand; in her left hand are riches and honor. Her ways are pleasant ways, and all her paths are peace. She is a tree of life to those who take hold of her, and happy are all who hold her fast.

Proverbs 3:13-18

● Promise—How Is Wisdom Obtained?

But if any of you lacks wisdom, let him ask of God, who gives to all men generously and without reproach, and it will be given to him. But let him ask in faith without any doubting, for the one who doubts is like the surf of the sea, driven and tossed by the wind. For let not that man expect that he will receive anything from the Lord, being a double-minded man, unstable in all his ways.

James 1:5-8

● Precaution—Are There Warnings about Wisdom?

Thus says the Lord, "Let not a wise man boast of his wisdom, and let not the mighty man boast of his might, let not a rich man boast of his riches; but let him who boasts boast of this, that he understands and knows Me, that I am the Lord who exercises lovingkindness, justice, and righteousness on earth; for I delight in these things," declares the Lord.

Jeremiah 9:23-24

● Paradox—Are There Surprises with Wisdom?

Let no man deceive himself. If any man among you thinks that he is wise in this age, let him become foolish that he may become wise.

1 Corinthians 3:18

● Practice—What Should We Do with Wisdom?

Therefore be careful how you walk, not as unwise men, but as wise, making the most of your time, because the days are evil. So then do not be foolish, but understand what the will of the Lord is.

Ephesians 5:15-17

Wisdom's Fruit

Who among you is wise and understanding? Let him show by his good behavior his deeds in the gentleness of wisdom. But if you have bitter jealousy and selfish ambition in your heart, do not be arrogant and so lie against the truth. This wisdom is not that which comes down from above, but is earthly, natural, demonic. For where jealousy and selfish ambition exist, there is disorder and every evil thing.

But the wisdom from above is first pure, then peaceable, gentle, reasonable, full of mercy and good fruits, unwavering, without hypocrisy. And the seed whose fruit is righteousness is sown in peace by those who make peace.

James 3:13-18

James distinguished between an earthly wisdom and true godly wisdom from above. Wisdom from God will reflect good conduct with a gentle character, while the counterfeit wisdom of demons produces evil and disorder. Righteousness and peace accompany authentic wisdom. In verse 17, we see a kaleidoscope of wisdom patterns describing the transformed life of one who is spiritually mature in wisdom. James asked, "Who among you is wise and understanding?" in verse 13, and then provided the basis for determining the answer in verse 17.

● Pure. The premier feature of godly wisdom is cleanness or, put another way, the absence of sin's pollution. Wisdom and desire for sinlessness are synonymous. The church is to be pure like a chaste virgin (2 Cor. 11:2); Christians are to think on pure things (Phil. 4:8); young women are to be pure

(Titus 2:5); and leaders in the church need to keep pure (1 Tim. 5:22).

The ancient church father Tertullian put purity in perspective with his statement:

> *Be clothed with the silk of honesty, the fine linen of holiness and the purple of chastity; thus adorned, God will be your friend.*

As Christ wisely withstood the impure lure of sin, so should we (Matt. 4:1-11).

● Peaceable. Wisdom makes peace, not war. Peacemakers are called sons of God (Matt. 5:9). Peace is included in the fruit produced by God's Spirit (Gal. 5:22). We are to let the peace of Christ rule our hearts (Col. 3:15). Since Christ is called the "Prince of Peace" (Isa. 9:6), Christians need to be ambassadors of peace (2 Cor. 5:20).

● Gentle. The Greek word we translate "gentle" contains much more than our English word conveys. Let me try to fill it out with some descriptive phrases:

sweet reasonableness

going the second mile

not demanding one's rights

full of mercy

discerning between the letter and spirit of the law

Gentleness should characterize the elders' behavior in the church (1 Tim. 3:3). Believers need to be gentle with one another (Phil. 4:5). Ultimately, Christians are to be gentle with all men (Titus 3:2). As Christ wisely spoke gentle words to the thief, so should we to those who seek Christ (Luke 23:39-43).

● Reasonable. This makes us conciliatory and willing to yield when spiritual progress can be gained. If we are reasonable, no one will ever characterize us as "course grade sandpaper." Christ always yielded to His Heavenly Father; that's our example to follow.

I can do nothing on my own initiative. As I hear, I judge;

and My judgment is just, because I do not seek My own will, but the will of Him who sent Me.

John 5:30

● Full of Mercy. Since God is rich in mercy, so should we be (Eph. 2:4). By God's great mercy we were born again and made heirs of eternal life (1 Peter 1:3; Titus 3:5). Mercy withholds judgment and extends grace without violating justice. We can follow in the footsteps of Christ's full mercy, as extended to the harlot (John 8:1-11), and to Peter (John 21:17).

● Full of Good Fruits. The idea here is not so much fruit in character as fruit in action that qualifies to be called good. Like mercy, these fruits should flow in abundance.

The pattern that James calls for follows the teaching of Jesus who demanded fruit (John 15:2), *more* fruit (John 15:2), and *much* fruit (John 15:5, 8).

● Unwavering. With regard to the things of God, we are to be single-minded, without compromise, and consistent. If we don't waver, we won't be blown around by every wind of doctrine or trickery of men (Eph. 4:14). Like Christ, we should always pray,

Father, if Thou are willing, remove this cup from Me; yet not My will, but Thine be done.

Luke 22:42

● Without Hypocrisy. Sincere, genuine, unpretentious, and without a mask all describe this quality. Our love (Rom. 12:9) and our faith (1 Tim. 1:5) are to be without hypocrisy. What we claim to be we are to be. Just as Jesus claimed to be a servant (Matt. 20:28) and actually served (John 13:12-17), so we need to live with transparent honesty.

Wise Transformation

Job twice asked the significant question, "Where can wisdom be found; where does wisdom come from?" (Job 28:12, 20) He answered his own questions,

God understands its way; and He knows its place. For He looks to the ends of the earth, and sees everything under the heavens. When He imparted weight to the wind, and meted out the waters by measure, when He set a limit for the rain and a course for the thunderbolt, then He saw it and declared it; He established it and also searched it out. And to man He said, "Behold, the fear of the Lord, that is wisdom; and to depart from evil is understanding.

Job 28:23-28

So wisdom begins with the transformation wrought by salvation, but it does not end there.

Wisdom resides in God's Word (Ps. 19:7). By it believers are transformed with the renewing of their minds (Rom. 12:2). Going a step further, wisdom not only knows God's Word but obeys it.

The conclusion, when all has been heard, is: fear God and keep His commandments, because this applies to every person.

Ecclesiastes 12:13

True wisdom avoids being conformed to this world and its lusts (Rom. 12:2; 1 Peter 1:14), and rather pursues transformation into the image of our wise Savior.

But we all, with unveiled face beholding as in a mirror the glory of the Lord, are being transformed into the same image from glory to glory, just as from the Lord, the Spirit.

2 Corinthians 3:18

Acquiring Wisdom

For a true Christian, true spiritual wisdom comes by at least four means. First, we can ask God for wisdom. When Solomon could have anything he wanted from God, he asked for wisdom and discernment (1 Kings 3:3-9). God commended him because he did not ask for long life or riches but wisdom. Thus Solomon became the wisest man of history (1 Kings

4:29-34). This same invitation to pray for wisdom awaits us today.

But if any of you lacks wisdom, let him ask of God, who gives to all men generously and without reproach, and it will be given to him. But let him ask in faith without any doubting, for the one who doubts is like the surf of the sea driven and tossed by the wind. For let not that man expect that he will receive anything from the Lord, being a double-minded man, unstable in all his ways.

James 1:5-8

Second, wisdom can also be obtained from God's Word (Ps. 19:7). God's invitation to this source is also available to all.

Let the Word of Christ richly dwell within you.

Colossians 3:16

Third, wisdom closely associates itself with the Holy Spirit. Bezalel was filled with the Spirit of God in wisdom (Ex. 31:3) as were the seven servants of the early church (Acts 6:3). Thus, to be filled with the Holy Spirit corresponds to being filled with wisdom.

Fourth, the crowds marveled at Christ's wisdom (Matt. 13:54; Mark 6:2). Luke reports He increased in wisdom (2:40, 52). Thus as we abide in Christ (John 15:4-7), we abide in wisdom.

Christian spirituality involves growing to be like God in character and conduct through *the transforming work* of God's Word and God's Spirit.

Consecrate me now to Thy service, Lord,
By the pow'r of grace divine;
Let my soul look up with a steadfast hope,
And my will be lost in Thine.[1]

8
THE FREEDOM OF SUBMISSION

During the time of the Czars in Russia, one of the Czars walked out of his palace into the garden where he found a sentry walking in front of a plot of weeds. He asked the soldier, "Why are you here? What are you guarding?"

The sentry said, "Sir, I do not know. I have been told that this is my post and I am serving faithfully."

The Czar thought that was strange, and so he went to the captain of the watch and asked him, "What are they guarding?" The captain replied, "Sir, I know not what they are guarding, but we have done it for years."

That still seemed strange to the Czar, so he asked that the post be investigated. They delved back into history and discovered that 100 years before, Catherine the Great was given a rosebush as a gift. She planted it in that place and asked for a sentry so that the plot would not be overrun by people.

Six months later, the rosebush died, but the post continued on for another 99 ½ years until somebody asked the strategic question: Why? What is the reason for it? For 99 ½ years, a weed-infested bed that had no purpose to anyone was guarded by the best of the Russian Army!

I pray that when we stand before God in heaven that kind of experience will not have been true in our lives. We don't want to have to answer God's question, "Why did you do this?" with "Sir, I do not know, but I have done it that way for years and did not think to ask why." To avoid such a possibility, let's go back to Scripture and rediscover our original marching instructions.

The Principle of Paradox

While most people would question their paradoxical connection, freedom and submission belong together. Think about it! If I submit to the law of gravity, I will be able to live freely; but an attempt to free myself from it could lead to a moment of instant exhilaration and then sudden death.

Scripture abounds with kingdom paradoxes. Let me remind you of a few. "But many who are first will be last; and the last, first" (Mark 10:31). "Whoever wishes to be great among you shall be your servant" (Mark 10:43; see also Matt. 23:11). "Whoever wishes to be the first among you must be the slave of all" (Mark 10:44). "Whoever then humbles himself as this child, he is the greatest in the kingdom of heaven" (Matt. 18:4). "For he who is least among you, this is the one who is great" (Luke 9:48).

Before we became Christians, we were dead in our sins and trespasses (Eph. 2:1) but after salvation, although now alive with Christ (Eph. 2:5), we are dead to sin (Rom. 6:11).

Somehow it's Christ who lives my Christian life (Gal. 2:20); yet at the same time I too live my Christian life.

The most important of these apparent contradictions, however, is the spiritual paradox between freedom and slavery.

For when you were slaves of sin, you were free in regard to righteousness. . . . But now having been freed from sin and enslaved to God, you derive your benefit, resulting in sanctification, and the outcome, eternal life.

Romans 6:20, 22

We have been freed from the bondage of obedience to sin, and concurrently enslaved to God's righteous authority in our lives. This paradox is nowhere more evident than in the New Testament texts which refer to Christians as servants, slaves, or bondservants. True liberation comes from enslavement to God's kingdom. As such, we were freed (saved) to serve the Lord of lords and King of kings.

For they themselves report about us what kind of a reception we had with you, and how you turned to God from idols to serve a living and true God.

1 Thessalonians 1:9

The corollary paradox simply put is this, "We distinguish ourselves as servants by what we are becoming in character, and by constancy of mature, Christian lifestyle, rather than by the deeds we perform."

This truth found its fullest expression in Paul's instructions to Timothy for the Ephesian church. We'll be looking at a passage which gives qualifications for those seeking a church office but which, in fact, sets the character standard for the paradoxical phenomenon of being a servant and thereby being free to honor Christ in the church.

A Preview

First Timothy 3:8-13 explains God's servantship pattern for the church, but its application really extends to all Christians. This is the pattern of living which God commends to us.

Deacons likewise must be men of dignity, not double-tongued or addicted to much wine or fond of sordid gain, but holding to the mystery of the faith with a clear conscience. And let these also first be tested; then let them serve as deacons if they are beyond reproach. Women must like-

wise be dignified, not malicious gossips, but temperate, faithful in all things. Let deacons be husbands of only one wife and good managers of their children and their own households. For those who have served well as deacons obtain for themselves a high standing and great confidence in the faith that is in Christ Jesus.

These six verses contain what God intends the church to know about a servant/slave of Jesus Christ. What makes this text so important? Why is this passage so different than any of the other New Testament texts on servanthood?

It is true that the New Testament has much to say about serving. There are four different words for serving—*doulos,* normally translated bondslave; I own nothing and I am owned by someone else (Rom. 6:16); *hupēretēs,* an under rower, a third-level galley slave and rower (that's about as low as you can get; Paul calls himself that in 1 Cor. 4:1); *leiturgos,* which has to do with spiritual service to God; it might be used of one who served in a priestly function (Acts 13:2); and *diakonos,* just a simple table waiter, one who does the menial tasks of life (1 Tim. 3:8, 12).

Since these four words are used over 250 times in the New Testament, it is safe to say that servanthood is a major thread in the Gospel. Jesus modeled servanthood for all. He said that He did not come to be served, but to serve (Matt. 20:28). He also said, "The greatest among you shall be your servant" (Matt. 23:11).

All Christians, without exception, are gifted to serve. Peter said, "As each one has received a special gift, employ it in serving one another" (1 Peter 4:10). Scripture reports that God gave apostles, prophets, evangelists, and pastor-teachers for the equipping of the saints—that is, you and me—for the work of service to the building up of the body of Christ (Eph. 4:11-12).

Scripture commands us all to serve. Paul wrote in Galatians 5:13, "Through love serve one another."

All those who have been brought into the family of God by His grace are to be servants.

The Prototype

Let's look at the prototype for servantship in Acts 6. Here, the church was in its infant stage. Babies grow "like Topsy" and are not sure where they are headed. Acts 5:42 reports that while the church was teaching and preaching Jesus as the Christ, and the disciples were increasing in number, even while there was great joy in the church, there was a complaint.

This complaint arose on the part of the Hellenistic Jews against the native Hebrews. Those who were Greek by birth, but Jewish by religious preference, said that their widows were being overlooked in the daily serving of food. It had nothing to do with doctrine per se, but it had everything to do with the essential albeit mundane task of who got fed and who got the most.

So the apostles summoned the congregation and said, "It is not desirable for us to neglect the Word of God in order to serve tables" (6:2). They were setting priorities in the church.

I don't believe for a minute that they would have minded putting their hands in soapy dishwater to clean up the plates, or donning an apron and cooking food and serving it. But they knew that doing so would cause them to neglect the Word of God. If we have to choose between food for the body and food for the soul, food for the soul always comes first.

So they said, "We have a problem. We have more ministry than we have men, so we have to expand the leadership corps to get the job done."

They went to the congregation and said, in effect, "We as apostles delegate to you the responsibility of selecting from among you seven men of good reputation, full of the Spirit and of wisdom, whom we may put in charge of this task" (6:3). They meant, "We are going to need some more people to come alongside and help us, because it is important that we feed all the widows, so that there be no complaining in the church."

The apostles concluded, "We will devote ourselves to prayer and to the ministry of the Word of God" (6:4). The statement found approval with the whole congregation. They knew the apostles and they knew God worked through them, so they chose Stephen, a man full of faith and of the Holy Spirit, along with Philip, Prochorus, Nicanor, Timon, Parmenas, and Nicolas, a proselyte from Antioch.

Then these men came before the apostles, and after praying, the apostles laid their hands on them. I love what it says in verse 7. As people were in tune with the Spirit of God and were committed to the priority of God, "the Word of God kept on spreading." The number of the disciples continued to increase greatly in Jerusalem, and a great many of the priests became obedient to the faith.

Early on, the apostles discovered that they couldn't do it all. So the initial leadership of the church consisted of apostles and those servants called out of the congregation and delegated by the apostles to serve with them. That is the prototype of the pattern the church later developed.

God's Pattern for Men

The model for servanthood in the church starts with a person displaying a habitual lifestyle of Christian maturity. The classic biblical passage that outlines these character qualities is 1 Timothy 3:8-13. This passage talks about those who would serve as deacons and deaconesses in the church, special servants who were recognized because they modeled mature Christianity. These standards then stand as a measure of maturity for all Christians.

Verses 8-9 and 11 contain seven qualities of a servant. Verse 11 gives four qualities which really summarize those previous seven. As you look at the pattern for servanthood, ask yourself, "How am I doing?"

● Servants must be marked by dignity. That doesn't mean that they dress in a three-piece suit and wear wing-tips all the time. It doesn't mean they sleep in a tie. Dignity has nothing to do with their outward appearance. It has everything to do with how they are dressed on the inside. The *King James Version* calls them "men who are grave." That doesn't mean that servants walk around with a big frown on their faces, but that they are people who have respectability and dignity.

I like the *New International Version* translation. It calls them people "worthy of respect because of who they are." They are noble. They are honorable. They are responsible. That quality is for all Christians. It is the way mature, older men are to be and the way they are to teach younger men to be, according to Titus 2:2. To sum it up, it is *maturity that commands respect.*

• Servants are not only to be men of dignity, maturity, worthy of respect, but they also are not to be double-tongued. Literally, they are not to engage in double-talk, but to be consistent in their living.

That is why the *New International Version* translates this simply as "sincere." Such people say what they mean and mean what they say. They are not looking out for their own advantage but are asking, "How can we advance the church?"

• Servants are "not addicted to much wine." Servants are not only worthy of respect because of their maturity and their consistency, but also because they are being controlled by God's Spirit and not by some outside influence.

In our day and age, there are all sorts of control problems beyond alcohol, such as drugs, for instance. The point is that those who have the serious responsibility to serve need to be in total control of their senses. Their minds need to be clear. They need to be full of energy and totally controlled by God's Spirit. This is why it says in Ephesians 5:18, "Do not get drunk with wine, for that is dissipation, but be filled with the Spirit"—not distilled spirits but the Divine Spirit.

• Servants should not be "fond of sordid gain." In twenti-eth-century lingo, they are not to be money-grubbers, but are to be more interested in the things of God than the things of earth. That is why Jesus said, "But seek first His kingdom and His righteousness; and all these things shall be added to you" (Matt. 6:33).

By the way, this same quality applies for elders or pastors. In Titus 1:11 we read that overseers should not work in the church "for the sake of sordid gain," "greedy for filthy lucre," says the *King James Version.* Money is never to be the object of ministry. A person with an unhealthy outlook on money will either neglect the ministry or pervert it for money.

● Servants are to hold to the mystery of the faith with a clear conscience. What does this mean? Very simply, that they are to have a firm grasp on, and an unfaltering allegiance to, the Word of God. They believe that it came from God through men and was written down accurately in the original autographs, and that all within it is truth to be obeyed.

What did Paul mean by "the mystery of the faith"? He meant that we would not know the mystery unless God revealed it to us. That which has been revealed by God is to be grasped firmly by those who would serve. They are to be doctrinally sound and not confused. Also, they are to serve with a clear conscience.

They are to believe in their hearts what they have affirmed with their lips; and what they believe, they are to live out in the servantship of the church. There is to be no shallow veneer of outward spirituality without inward scriptural substance.

Later on Paul tells us something of what that mystery of the faith is, for he says "by common confession, great is the mystery of godliness" (3:16). This is talking about the incarnation of Christ.

He who was revealed in the flesh,
was vindicated in the Spirit,
beheld by angels,
proclaimed among the nations,
believed on in the world,
taken up in glory.

Servants don't let go if things get a little rough. They will hold on even if it causes the loss of their lives. That is what a slave is to be, according to God's standard.

In Acts 6, when they selected those seven men full of wisdom and full of the Spirit of God, do you remember who was first on the list? It was Stephen. It says that Stephen went forth and ministered great signs, wonders, and miracles in the power of God. Later in Acts 7 he preached a fantastic message, so powerful that it convicted the Jews until they took up stones to kill him.

• Servants are to be the husband of only one wife. It says the same thing in 3:2 for elders. For all servants, God has the same standard for the home. You are to be a one-woman man. Women, you are to be a one-man woman. You are not to have eyes for anyone else, but are to be wholly devoted to your mate.

The greatest cure for immorality and adultery is, first, to be deeply in love with Jesus Christ; and, second, if you are married, to be deeply growing in love with your partner.

• Servants will be good managers of their children and of their own households. They must have a demonstrated ability to be servants/leaders of their families.

Those are the seven qualities given for men: dignified, not double-tongued, not given to much wine, not fond of sordid gain, holding firmly to the mystery of the faith with a clear conscience, having eyes only for his wife, and maintaining a good reputation as a leader in the home.

When God said that servants must qualify in this pattern of life, He was talking about direction, about lifestyle, about consistency in one who would be a servant of Jesus Christ.

God's Pattern for Women
Paul went on to speak about women servants (3:11). The text says, "Women must likewise—" If you have the *King James Version,* it says "wives." That is an unfortunate translation, because Paul was not talking about the wives of deacons, but about women qualified to serve in the church.

The little word "likewise" is referring back to 3:8. Just as deacons are to be qualified, as elders are to be qualified, so are deaconesses. The Greek noun *diakonos* has a masculine gender, but that has nothing to do with the sex of a person. There is no female form of *diakonos.*

There are only four qualities listed in verse 11. But let me suggest that there is not a lesser standard for women than for men. Paul just decided to be a little briefer.

• Women must likewise be dignified. He uses the same word that he did in verse 8. Women must also be worthy of respect because of their maturity.

• Women are not to be malicious gossips. The Greek noun is *diabolos,* the word translated "devil" in the New Testament. He says they are not to be devil-like in their conversation—slandering, starting rumors and with their tongues setting fires that righteousness can't put out. So the tongue of a deacon and the tongue of a deaconess are incredibly important.

• Women are to be temperate. This word was used for elders in 1 Timothy 3:2, who were also to be temperate or sober, that is, moderate, balanced, and clear-headed; it would encompass all that he has already said about wine and money in relation to the deacon in verse 8.

• Women were to be "faithful in all things"—faithful with regard to the home and to their relationship to family.

Examine Yourself

How do we recognize a mature servant? What is the ultimate test? Verse 10 says, "Let these also first be tested." How does one become a deacon or deaconess? There is a twofold process: let them first be tested, and then let them serve.

To grow in the grace and knowledge of the Lord Jesus Christ is the mandate of every Christian. It is important that you cultivate the qualities of Christ in your life. Some of you feel that if you aspire to leadership, it is yours to go for. Others think you can sit back and fold your arms and say, "Let somebody else do it, I'll be just a second-class citizen in the kingdom of God."

We recognize in our assemblies those who are maturing to become like Christ. Let them cultivate the qualities of Christ, and then let them submit themselves for testing and affirmation.

It is kind of like a take-home exam. There are no trick questions and no surprises. It is obvious what God's standards are, and you can take the test as many times as you want to. Look at what it says: "Let them first be tested and then let them serve as deacons if they are found blameless." Paul's point is not perfection, but a consistent, obvious, outward pattern demonstrated over a long enough time. Then people can determine if spiritual maturity is real.

I'm amazed it doesn't talk about giftedness. It doesn't say, "If you can speak well," "If you teach kids well," or "If you can do this or that." It talks about who you are, about godly character, about being beyond reproach.

This is where churches go astray. Most churches which are committed to the Word of God appoint someone to be a deacon or deaconess and believe that by the appointment he or she will become a servant. God's Word indicates that this is backward. They are first to be tested and only if they pass the test are they to be chosen. Never is the church to choose and then test. It is to test, pass, and choose. If you have been in many churches, you know that once a person gets a deacon or deaconess badge, they don't want to give it back!

Let me tell you what a deacon is in the church of God—just a simple table waiter. Deacons are not the people at the table eating the food and paying for it. They are just the waiters. They constantly go into the kitchen and come out, serve the people, go back into the kitchen. It's tiring and laborious. There is nothing glorious about it from an earthly perspective. But deacons have a heart to serve God in the midst of God's people; they are godly in their character, and they live out Jesus Christ in their lives.

The Prize
We have seen the prototype, that is, how God began that pattern and worked it out until it became the normal pattern of the church. There is to be testing. And for those who submit themselves and pass the test, there is a real prize.

Maybe some of you are asking, "Is it worth it? Should I go through all this? I'll make myself too vulnerable if I do that! What if I don't pass?"

There is no shame in not passing. It just means that you

need to grow a little more. The only shame is if there is no desire in your heart or mind to grow in Christ. It is not a shame to be an infant, is it? We don't go around saying, "Look at all those shameful kids in the nursery. They wear diapers and I am in big people's clothes!" There is no shame, as long as I am becoming what God wants me to be.

What is the prize? I love verse 13, for it says that those who have served well, rightly, correctly, acceptably, and commendably unto God as deacons and deaconesses, receive a high standing. I don't think it is talking so much about a high standing in the presence of God as a high standing in the assembly of God's people. We have submitted ourselves to an incredibly rigorous test and having made ourselves vulnerable, we have passed the test.

Jesus said that if you want to be high in the assembly, you go low. If you want to soar, you dive. If you want to be first, be last. If you want to be a lord, be a servant. If you want a high standing in the assembly, don't go up—go down. That is the freedom of submission.

There is a second prize that He gives that is perhaps even greater. You will obtain a great confidence in the faith that is in Christ Jesus. Nothing is more exhilarating, nothing will better launch you to more growth than to learn that the Bible works, to experience the walk of faith, and to know that the greatest spiritual freedom comes to the most committed servants of Jesus Christ.

Holy, holy, holy!
Lord God Almighty!
Early in the morning
Our song shall rise to Thee;
Holy, holy, holy!
Merciful and mighty!
God in three Persons,
Blessed Trinity![1]

9
BOTTOM-LINE SPIRITUALITY

One of our fine students at The Master's Seminary sent me this touching letter.

Dear Dr. Mayhue,

The past six months of my life have been a time of great learning for me. God used many circumstances in my life to show me why I need to depend on Him much more than I do. However, in the midst of the learning, I found myself lacking motivation for the task (preparation in seminary) God has called me to. It seemed as if the harder I tried to "get back on track," the worse things became. I would ask myself what happened to the desire I once had; how could I not do my best, when men's lives depend on it?

Over the holidays, I had a chance to reflect on some of these events; and God made clear to me the reason behind the struggles I faced. Simply put, I had misplaced my priorities. By that I mean I had fallen into the tragedy of placing seminary and ministry before communing with our Divine Father. Yes, I still spent time with God; however, the time was not the consecrated communion I have enjoyed in the past.

What a fool I was to allow such a thing to happen. However, our gracious Father has shown to me the steps I need to take to prevent it from happening again. I believe seminary is helpful; however, nothing can ever better prepare a man for serving the King than consistent and consecrated communion before His throne. Ministry is the reason for our pilgrimage on earth, but ministry placed before our "First Love" is vain. [2]

He poignantly expressed the regret that the spiritual character being formed *in* him had not manifested itself fully by emerging *out* of him in his spiritual conduct and communion with God. I suspect that most of us have needed to write more than one letter like this in our Christian life.

If he had asked, "How can I tell when I'm back on track?" I would have directed his thoughts to Psalm 15. We need to look there too.

O Lord, who may abide in Thy tent?
Who may dwell on Thy holy hill?
He who walks with integrity, and works righteousness,
And speaks truth in his heart.
He does not slander with his tongue,
Nor does evil to his neighbor,
Nor takes up a reproach against his friend;
In whose eyes a reprobate is despised,
But who honors those who fear the Lord;
He swears to his own hurt, and does not change;
He does not put out his money at interest,
Nor does he take a bribe against the innocent.
He who does these things will never be shaken.

Psalm 15 does not speak to the fact of salvation but, rather, to the fruit of redemption. It spells out the unchanging desire and standard of God for His redeemed children to be transformed into His never-changing character which is summed up in *holiness.*

When the character of God really begins to shape a person's life, what does it look like in us? The psalmist lays out three major characteristics to authenticate genuine, growing, godly character and conduct in the life of a true believer.

The Right Concern

O Lord, who may abide in Thy tent?
Who may dwell on Thy holy hill?

Psalm 15:1

To the psalmist and prophets in the tenth century B.C., these questions would produce immediate thoughts of the tabernacle on Mt. Zion where the Israelites worshiped. The two terms "tent" and "holy hill" signified God's presence over the ark of the covenant (Ex. 25:22). Located in the holy of holies, the ark of the covenant was where the Shekinah glory of God dwelt. For every true worshiper of God, this represented the most sacred spot on earth. The psalmist begins with this inquiry, "Who is qualified to stand in the presence of the Lord?"

The tent of meeting or tabernacle is where God's people met God (Ex. 25). It accompanied the Jews as they wandered in the wilderness and went to battle with them when Joshua captured the Promised Land (Josh. 6:8). Hundreds of years later it found its rightful place in Jerusalem under King David's leadership (2 Sam. 5-6).

God's "tent" rested on a holy hill where a holy God was to be worshiped by a holy people. This "hill" finds prominent mention in the Psalms (2:6; 3:4; 24:3; 43:3-4; 74:2; 99:9).

When Moses stood in the presence of God in the wilderness, the Lord told him, "Remove your sandals from your feet, for the place on which you are standing is holy ground" (Ex. 3:5). When faced with God's holiness, the Prophet Isaiah cried out, "Woe is me, for I am ruined! Because I am a man of unclean lips, and I live among a people of unclean lips; for my eyes have seen the King, the Lord of hosts" (Isa. 6:5). Both of these men experienced the essence of the question voiced in Psalm 15:1, and they understood God's uncompromising demand for holy behavior.

As obedient children, do not be conformed to the former lusts which were yours in your ignorance, but like the Holy One who called you, be holy yourselves also in all your behavior; because it is written, "You shall be holy, for I am holy."

1 Peter 1:14-16

This thought of standing or dwelling in the presence of God is one of the great unifying themes of Scripture. This marks the beginning point for the psalmist—seeking God on His terms, not ours. Whatever qualifies a person to abide in God's sacred tabernacle and to dwell on His holy hill must be decided by God, not by us. So the psalmist asks the appropriate question of the right Person when he begins, "O Lord...."

The Right Conduct

Some have asked, "Does Psalm 15 teach salvation by works?" Let me answer emphatically, "No!" This psalm beautifully portrays the fruit of sanctification in the life of one who is already saved. It pictures a person who submits to God's instructions on holiness and begins to exhibit the character qualities of God in his own personal life.

There are at least three good reasons to strongly insist that this psalm pictures the life of an authentic believer. First, the Old Testament teaches that salvation is by grace without human works (Joel 2:32; see Rom. 10:13). Second, the New Testament teaches identically the same truth (Eph. 2:8-10; Titus 3:5-7). Third, Psalms 13 and 14 teach salvation by God's doing, not by man's works.

The gracious overarching answer to the question of Psalm 15:1 is found in the following verse.

He who walks with integrity, and works righteousness,
And speaks truth in his heart.

Psalm 15:2

The psalmist pinpoints a person's walk, works, and words as the key elements. They will be seen in the integrity of one's life, the righteousness of one's labor, and the truthfulness of one's speech.

Psalm 24:3-4 develops the same theme in different phrasing.

Psalm 15:2	Psalm 24:4
walks with integrity	pure heart
works righteousness	clean hands
speaks truth	no falsehood

"How does this flesh out in everyday life?" As if anticipating our question, the psalmist continues and outlines the details in three arenas of life.

● The Interpersonal Arena. *"He does not slander with his tongue"* (15:3a). Our dealings with people are not to be characterized by slander or backbiting (Gal. 5:15), for a slanderer will not see the salvation of God (Ps. 50:20-23). We should never bless God and turn right around and curse men (James 3:9-10). James states strongly, "My brethren, these things ought not to be this way."

The Hebrew word for "slander" literally means "to walk about." We are not to have walking tongues that bear slanderous tales about other people. This instruction is not unique to Psalm 15.

Let no unwholesome word proceed from your mouth, but only such a word as is good for edification according to the need of the moment, that it may give grace to those who hear.

Ephesians 4:29

If anyone thinks himself to be religious, and yet does not bridle his tongue but deceives his own heart, this man's religion is worthless.

James 1:26

In our conversation, we are to be like the Lord Jesus Christ of whom it is written, "And all were speaking well of Him, and wondering at the gracious words which were falling from His lips" (Luke 4:22).

"Nor does evil to his neighbor" (15:3b). Unlike what Ahab did to Naboth (1 Kings 21), or David to Uriah (2 Sam. 11), or Haman to Mordecai (Esther 2–7), we are to do good to our neighbor.

But who is our neighbor? Jesus defined neighbor as anyone in the normal sphere of our life who is in need of mercy (Luke 10:25-37). So we are not surprised to read repeatedly in Scripture, "Love your neighbor as yourself" (Lev. 19:18; Matt. 22:39; Rom. 13:9-10; Gal. 5:14).

The psalmist warns, "Whoever secretly slanders his neighbor, him I will destroy" (Ps. 101:5). "Do not devise harm against your neighbor," warns the writer of Proverbs (3:29). We are to be like Jesus who looked at people with compassion (Matt. 9:36).

"Nor takes up a reproach against his friend" (15:3c). The psalmist has moved from people in general to a neighbor, and now to a close, intimate acquaintance. Proverbs variously describes a "friend" as one who loves at all times (17:17); who sticks closer than a brother (18:24); and whose wounds are faithfully designed to help not destroy (27:6). A friend is one who walks into your life when the others walk out.

The Hebrew word for "reproach" means "to scorn or treat with contempt." Rather, we are to treat our friends with respect and a desire to build up, not to tear down. If we are faithful to our friendships, then we will be like our Lord who befriended the sinners and publicans for whose sins He would die (Matt. 11:19), who befriended Peter who denied Him three times (John 21:15-23), and who befriended Thomas even though he doubted (John 20:26-29).

● The Spiritual Arena. *"In whose eyes a reprobate is despised"* (15:4a). At first glance this may sound as if it contradicts the love of God and seems overly harsh; yet, Jesus condemned the Pharisees (Matt. 23) and cleansed the temple twice (John 2; Matt. 21). So, there is a right kind of despising.

A "reprobate" is one who has rejected God and the things of God as utterly worthless. Therefore, we who value God most highly are to reject the reprobate's conclusions about God as worthless and untrue, and the reprobate's lifestyle as destructive and without value. In terms of our behavior toward them, listen to another psalm.

How blessed is the man who does not walk
in the counsel of the wicked,
Nor stand in the path of sinners,
Nor sit in the seat of scoffers!
But his delight is in the law of the Lord,
And in His law he meditates day and night.

Psalm 1:1-2

Does this mean we are not to evangelize the wicked? No—quite the opposite! We are to tell them about their sins and our holy Savior, but we are not to walk in their ungodly footsteps. Jesus best exemplifies this in Mark 2:15-17. After being criticized by the religious establishment for socializing with publicans and sinners, He responded, "I did not come to call the righteous, but sinners."

"But who honors those who fear the Lord" (15:4b). We are to love the brethren (Heb. 13:1). Those who fear the Lord share the same concern for standing in the presence of God because they have confessed and repented of their sin, and then have embraced the Lord Jesus Christ in His death, burial, and resurrection. Thus they now walk in His way (Ps. 128:1) and keep His commandments (Ecc. 12:13). Fearing God has become a lifestyle for them (Prov. 23:17; Col. 3:22; 1 Peter 2:17).

We are to treat our brothers and sisters (James 2:15) in the Lord with honor and love (John 1:12; Rom. 8:14, 16). We share the same faith (Rom. 8:15); we are fellow-heirs (Rom. 8:17); we all have one Father (Eph. 4:6); we have all been adopted (Eph. 1:5); we were all unworthy (Rom. 3:23); we were all saved the same way (Eph. 2:8-10); and we all were saved for the same ultimate purpose (Eph. 2:10; 1 Cor. 10:31).

Jesus manifested this quality of honoring others. A striking example was when He commended the widow for giving her two mites (Luke 21:1-4). And John reports, "Jesus knowing that His hour had come . . . having loved His own who were in the world, He loved them to the end" (John 13:1).

● The Community Arena. The psalmist has looked at the key lifestyle indicators that evidence an inward quest for holiness. They lie in the realm of interpersonal relationships and spiritual relationships and, finally, in community relationships.

"He swears to his own hurt, and does not change" (15:4c). Honesty marks the man of holiness who purposes never to be guilty of perjury in the courtroom of God. He knows that the Lord hates a lying tongue (Prov. 6:17). He commits himself to total truth and honesty, even when he will lose or be hurt by it.

Scripture clearly teaches the premium that God places on truth. We need to put deceiving lips away (Prov. 4:24); if we do not, our lies will be punished (Prov. 19:5, 9).

Jesus described Himself as "the truth" (John 14:6). When the soldiers maliciously approached Him in Gethsemane, He did not hedge, but rather forthrightly acknowledged that He was Jesus of Nazareth (John 18:1-9). When being tried before Pilate and Herod, instead of pleading the Fifth Amendment or using some other legal ploy to avoid the truth, He answered directly, and they crucified Him for it.

The writer of Proverbs gives us a great little prayer which I retreat to often, "Keep deception and lies far from me" (30:8).

"He does not put out his money at interest" (15:5a). This is not necessarily an anti-banking verse. Jesus affirmed normal business dealings involving interest (Luke 7:40-43; Matt. 25:14-30). However, it is a strong condemnation of charging usurious interest rates that take advantage of the poor.

In ancient times, the rich really did get richer and the poor much poorer. Exorbitant interest rates of 33 percent or even 50 percent were not uncommon. In some cases, double interest was charged whereby people had to pay interest on the original interest. These gouging rates would be charged for the barest necessities of life such as food, clothing, and shelter.

The Old Testament clearly prohibited the practice of charging interest to fellow Jews (Ex. 22:25-27; Lev. 25:35-38; Deut. 23:19-20). The basic meaning of the Hebrew word translated "at interest" is "to bite with the intention of hurting." In effect, the psalmist says, "Those of you who are rich, because you have more than the basics, do not grow more prosperous by making money at the expense of those who do not even have enough to survive." Of our Lord it is written,

For you know the grace of our Lord Jesus Christ, that though He was rich, yet for your sake He became poor, that you through His poverty might become rich.

2 Corinthians 8:9

"He does not take a bribe against the innocent" (15:5b). Men who can be bribed to condemn the innocent are labeled "worthless" in Scripture (1 Kings 21:10, 13). Those who bribe deserve to be called "evil" (1 Kings 21:17-26). The ultimate bribe was paid to Judas, the son of perdition, who betrayed the Lord Jesus Christ (Matt. 26:14-16; 27:1-5).

Jesus exemplified this prohibition in His life. Satan attempted to bribe Him with the promise of bypassing the cross and immediately ruling the world, if He would just denounce God the Father and worship Satan (Matt. 4:8-9). With this curt reply, "Begone, Satan!" (4:10), Jesus put Satan on notice that He could not be bought.

The Right Confidence

"He who does these things will never be shaken" (15:5c). No verse in Scripture states more clearly how one can personally be assured of the genuineness of salvation.

One whose salvation is real has every right to be continually confident about an abiding relationship with God and to feel certain that he qualifies to abide in God's tabernacle and stand on the Lord's holy hill (15:1). The psalms elsewhere echo this same blessed truth.

I have set the Lord continually before me;
Because He is at my right hand, I will not be shaken.

Psalm 16:8

For the king trusts in the Lord,
And through the lovingkindness of the Most High
he will not be shaken.

Psalm 21:7

He only is my rock and my salvation,
My stronghold; I shall not be greatly shaken.

Psalm 62:2

The outward marks of spiritual maturity which validate the inner character of holiness that comes through God's regenerating work in the life of a sinner include:

- A concern to seek God's holiness.
- A conduct submitted to God's standards of holiness.
- A confidence in the assurance of salvation brought about by habitually living out God's holiness.

PART TWO

THE CHRISTIAN'S PRACTICE

We need to warn such persons that there is no shortcut to holiness. It must be the business of their whole lives to grow in grace and continually to add one virtue to another. It is, as far as possible, "to go on towards perfection" (Hebrews 6:1). "He only that doeth righteousness is righteous" (1 John 3:7). Unless they bring forth "the fruit of the Spirit" (Galatians 5:22), they can have no sufficient evidence that they have actually received the Spirit of Christ, "without which they are none of His" (Romans 8:9). Unless, then, the root of the matter is not found in them, they are not adorning the doctrine of God, but disparaging and discrediting it.[1]

William Wilberforce

But, beloved, we are convinced of better things concerning you, and things that accompany salvation, though we are speaking in this way. For God is not unjust so as to forget your work and the love which you have shown toward His name, in having ministered and in still ministering to the saints. And we desire that each one of you show the same diligence so as to realize the full assurance of hope until the end, that you may not be sluggish, but imitators of those who through faith and patience inherit the promises.

Hebrews 6:9-12

Then in fellowship sweet
We will sit at His feet,
Or we'll walk by His side in the way;
What He says we will do,
Where He sends we will go—
Never fear, only trust and obey.[1]

10
SPIRITUAL CONDITIONING

Ben Johnson and Pete Rose share several life experiences. They are well-known athletes who disqualified themselves to participate in sports because they broke the rules. Parallels can be drawn to the Christian life, since the New Testament more than once compares the rigors of Christian living to disciplined athletic training and competition.

> *Therefore, since we have so great a cloud of witnesses surrounding us, let us also lay aside every encumbrance, and the sin which so easily entangles us, and let us run with endurance the race that is set before us, fixing our eyes on Jesus, the author and perfecter of faith, who for the joy set before Him endured the cross, despising the shame, and has sat down at the right hand of the throne of God.*
> *Hebrews 12:1-2*

Do you not know that those who run in a race all run, but only one receives the prize? Run in such a way that you may win. And everyone who competes in the games exercises self-control in all things. They then do it to receive a perishable wreath, but we an imperishable. Therefore I run in such a way, as not without aim; I box in such a way, as not beating the air; but I buffet my body and make it my slave, lest possibly, after I have preached to others, I myself should be disqualified.

1 Corinthians 9:24-27

Not that I have already obtained it, or have already become perfect, but I press on in order that I may lay hold of that for which also I was laid hold of by Christ Jesus. Brethren, I do not regard myself as having laid hold of it yet; but one thing I do: forgetting what lies behind and reaching forward to what lies ahead, I press on toward the goal for the prize of the upward call of God in Christ Jesus.

Philippians 3:12-14

But have nothing to do with worldly fables fit only for old women. On the other hand, discipline yourself for the purpose of godliness; for bodily discipline is only of little profit, but godliness is profitable for all things, since it holds promise for the present life and also for the life to come.

1 Timothy 4:7-8

And also if anyone competes as an athlete, he does not win the prize unless he competes according to the rules.

2 Timothy 2:5

Consistent spiritual victories, like a string of wins in sports, depend upon several factors. They include being experienced in using these disciplines.

- The discipline of conditioning—holiness cultivation
- The discipline of skill—spiritual growth
- The discipline of obedience—biblical submission
- The discipline of focus—spiritual priority

All these features come into play when Paul introduces us to a Christian way of life comprised of ten separate but vitally related elements. In keeping with an athletic motif, the apostle suggests "a Christian decathlon" of sorts. These ten events comprise the ABCs of Christian conditioning.

> *And we urge you, brethren, admonish the unruly, encourage the fainthearted, help the weak, be patient with all men. See that no one repays another with evil for evil, but always seek after that which is good for one another and for all men.*
>
> *Rejoice always; pray without ceasing; in everything give thanks; for this is God's will for you in Christ Jesus. Do not quench the Spirit; do not despise prophetic utterances. But examine everything carefully; hold fast to that which is good; abstain from every sort of evil.*
>
> *1 Thessalonians 5:14-22*

Assist the Spiritually Needy

> *And we urge you, brethren, admonish the unruly, encourage the fainthearted, help the weak, be patient with all men.*
> *1 Thessalonians 5:14*

Four kinds of people receive notice for the second time in this letter: *the unruly* (4:11-12); *the fainthearted* (4:13-18); *the weak* (4:1-8); and *all men* (3:12). These people are undisciplined, fearful, lacking strength, and unsaved.

The obligation to minister to them is a function of the entire body of believers. Every Christian needs to be involved, not just the pastor and other church leaders. Paul's strong urging assumes that "the brethren" have the spiritual resources lacking in these four groups. Christians in the body should be spiritually disciplined, courageous, strong, and true believers. Then they will be in a position to minister to those in need.

The first group involves the unruly or undisciplined, people who are "out of step" with the marching orders of Scripture.

Their lives tend to be anything but quiet, focused, and industrious. These folks do not take seriously 4:11-12:

Make it your business to lead a quiet life and attend to your own business and work with your hands, just as we commanded you; so that you may behave properly toward outsiders and not be in any need.

Believers are to lovingly confront or admonish these people to change their behavior. Paul illustrates this when he confronts a certain segment of the Thessalonians about their undisciplined and lazy ways (2 Thes. 3:6-12).

Those with "a small soul," the fainthearted or fearful, need encouragement or comfort. Paul demonstrates what he means in 1 Thessalonians 4:13-18 where he writes with truth and comfort concerning the destiny of loved ones who have already died. These words then are to be used in ministering to one another.

Mature believers are to hold onto those who are spiritually weak or lacking strength. They are to be a strength for those who might be morally weak (4:3-8). The best picture of this kind of ministry can be found in Paul's correspondence to the Corinthian church.

Finally, they are to be patient or endure with those who have not yet embraced Christ (all men). Long-suffering decidedly identifies one whom the Spirit controls (Gal. 5:22) and who characteristically loves people (1 Cor. 13:4). Paul prays that the Thessalonians will abound in love for unbelievers (3:12).

Be Concerned for the Good of Others

See that no one repays another with evil for evil, but always seek after that which is good for one another and for all men.

1 Thessalonians 5:15

Good, not evil, is to be the goal of our involvement with other people. No one is ever to seek evil as a repayment for evil; everyone is always to seek to do good for believers (one another) and unbelievers (all men) (see Gal. 6:10).

Jesus comments on this radical departure from normal human response in His great Sermon on the Mount.

You have heard that it was said, "An eye for an eye, and a tooth for a tooth." But I say to you, do not resist him who is evil; but whoever slaps you on your right cheek, turn to him the other also. And if anyone wants to sue you, and take your shirt, let him have your coat also. And whoever shall force you to go one mile, go with him two. Give to him who asks of you, and do not turn away from him who wants to borrow from you.

You have heard that it was said, "You shall love your neighbor, and hate your enemy." But I say to you, love your enemies, and pray for those who persecute you in order that you may be sons of your Father who is in heaven; for He causes His sun to rise on the evil and the good, and sends rain on the righteous and the unrighteous. For if you love those who love you, what reward have you? Do not even the tax-gatherers do the same? And if you greet your brothers only, what do you do more than others? Do not even the Gentiles do the same? Therefore you are to be perfect, as your heavenly Father is perfect.

Matthew 5:38-48

Paul, Peter, and John all echo the same idea.

Never pay back evil for evil to anyone. Respect what is right in the sight of all men. If possible, so far as it depends on you, be at peace with all men. Never take your own revenge, beloved, but leave room for the wrath of God, for it is written, "Vengeance is Mine, I will repay," says the Lord. "But if your enemy is hungry, feed him, and if he is thirsty, give him a drink; for in so doing you will heap burning coals upon his head." Do not be overcome by evil, but overcome evil with good.

Romans 12:17-21

To sum up, let all be harmonious, sympathetic, brotherly, kindhearted, and humble in spirit; not returning evil for evil, or insult for insult, but giving a blessing instead; for you were called for the very purpose that you might inherit a blessing.

1 Peter 3:8-9

Beloved, do not imitate what is evil, but what is good. The one who does good is of God; the one who does evil has not seen God.

3 John 11

By obeying these Scriptures, you will be a consistent doer of good and minimize the times you want to retaliate.

Cultivate a Joyful Heart

Rejoice always.

1 Thessalonians 5:16

If you are regularly assisting the spiritually needy and consistently concerned for the good of others, you will need to rejoice always in order to maintain your sanity.

Whether you're on top of life or underneath it, joy should be your constant companion (James 1:2-4). Joy in the Lord, even while you suffer, marks spiritual maturity (Pss. 31:7; 35:9; 40:16; 70:4).

But it is still my consolation, and I rejoice in unsparing pain, that I have not denied the words of the Holy One.

Job 6:10

Now I rejoice in my sufferings for your sake, and in my flesh I do my share on behalf of His body (which is the church) in filling up that which is lacking in Christ's afflictions.

Colossians 1:24

But to the degree that you share the sufferings of Christ, keep on rejoicing, so that also at the revelation of His glory, you may rejoice with exultation.

1 Peter 4:13

The focus of your joy should be on the Lord and the things of eternity. Here's a sample of biblically recommended objects for joy.

The mighty acts of God	Psalm 66:6
The name(s) of God	Psalm 89:16
The Word of God	Psalm 119:162
The salvation of God	Isaiah 61:10
The Holy Spirit of God	Romans 14:17

Paul put it most directly to the Philippians, "Rejoice in the Lord always; again, I will say, rejoice! (4:4)

Joy colored Paul and Barnabas' jail term in Philippi where they sang hymns of praise to God after they had been beaten and illegally incarcerated (Acts 16:25). For the joy set before Him, Jesus endured the cross (Heb. 12:2).

Depend on Prayer

Pray without ceasing.

1 Thessalonians 5:17

People who haven't made prayer a habit in good times won't usually pray in a crisis. The genius of Paul's exhortation lies in prayer's duration — "without ceasing." The idea is not that you are praying every single second of every hour, but rather that prayer is a consistent pattern in your life.

No one better exemplifies the consistency and resulting effect of unceasing prayer than Daniel. His professional enemies could find no fault with his life other than that he remained faithful to God (Dan. 6:4-5). So they persuaded the king to sign into law a mandate that only the king could be worshiped for the next thirty days. A trip to the lions' den would reward those who disobeyed. Look at Daniel's response:

Now when Daniel knew that the document was signed, he

entered his house (now in his roof chamber he had win-
dows open toward Jerusalem); and he continued kneeling
on his knees three times a day, praying and giving thanks
before his God, as he had been doing previously.

Daniel 6:10

He dared to continue his habit of prayer in the face of a
death threat. After an overnight stay with the lions, Daniel
lived while his accusers died (6:21-24).

Paul practiced what he preached. As you read his letters in
the New Testament, you see prayer as a common theme.
Paul prayed without ceasing (Rom. 1:9-10; 1 Cor. 1:4-9;
2 Cor. 13:7; Eph. 1:16; Phil. 1:4; Col. 1:3; 1 Thes. 1:2;
2 Thes. 1:3; 2 Tim. 1:3; and Phile. 4).

No one has equaled the regularity of our Lord in prayer.
He prayed in public at His baptism (Luke 3:21). Christ habitually prayed in solitude, whether it was in the wilderness or
the mountains—at times all night long (Luke 5:16; 6:12;
9:18). He took some of the disciples to pray on the mountain
(Luke 9:18-29). Later they asked Him to teach them how to
pray (Luke 11:1). He prayed for others (Luke 22:32) and for
Himself (Luke 22:41, 44).

Enter God's Gates with Thanksgiving

In everything give thanks; for this is God's will for you in
Christ Jesus.

1 Thessalonians 5:18

God's will demands that we live in a habitual state of thank-
fulness. Elsewhere Paul wrote, "always giving thanks for all
things" (Eph. 5:20). The psalmist said,

Enter His gates with thanksgiving,
And His courts with praise.
Give thanks to Him; bless His name.
For the Lord is good;
His lovingkindness is everlasting,

And His faithfulness to all generations.

Psalm 100:4-5

Whether in life or death, thanksgiving remains God's order of the day. When speaking of death, Paul wrote, "But thanks be to God, who gives us the victory through our Lord Jesus Christ" (1 Cor. 15:57).

As our Lord instituted the bread and cup which would symbolize His soon death for our sins, He gave thanks before partaking of both the bread and the cup (Mark 14:22-23; Luke 22:19-20).

To live maturely in Christ means to live with a "gratitude attitude."

Fire Up the Spirit

Do not quench the Spirit.

1 Thessalonians 5:19

The NIV translates this phrase, "Do not put out the Spirit's fire." The focus here is on the Spirit's activity in the life of a true believer. "Do not quench" appropriately responds to the picture of God's Spirit as fire (Acts 2:3).

How does one quench the Spirit? Very simply—with sin. As water is to fire, so sin is to God's Spirit working in us.

If I quench the Spirit, I will hate; if I walk in the Spirit, I will love. If we look at the fruit of the Spirit in Galatians 5:22-23, we can see the opposite effect of quenching the Spirit.

Fueled by the Spirit	Quenching the Spirit
Joy	Gloom
Peace	War
Patience	Anger
Kindness	Meanness
Goodness	Evil
Faithfulness	Selfishness
Gentleness	Malice
Self-control	Out of control

Paul contrasts these two ideas in Ephesians 4:30-32 as he commands the Ephesians to not grieve the Holy Spirit. Then he commands them to put away the kinds of attitudes and responses that are grievous to God (4:31). They include:

Bitterness	Clamor
Wrath	Slander
Anger	Malice

These attitudes need to be replaced with Spirit-generated qualities that mark out true spirituality and minimize the deeds of the flesh (4:32). Kindness, tenderheartedness, and forgiveness stand in contrast to meanness, hardheartedness, and vengefulness.

Give Prophetic Truth Honor

Do not despise prophetic utterances.

1 Thessalonians 5:20

Here Paul is talking about the authoritative words of God through a prophet. Prophecies can refer to the spoken word (1 Cor. 14:6; 1 Tim. 1:18; 4:14; Rev. 11:6), but more often it refers to the written Word of God.

The prophecy of Isaiah	Matthew 13:14-15
The prophecy of Scripture	2 Peter 1:20-21
Words of the prophecy	Revelation 1:3
Words of the prophecy of this book	Revelation 22:7, 10, 18-19

In Paul's day there were both. In our day we have neither kind of prophecy. The fruit of the historic prophetic ministry is what we call Scripture. So we could paraphrase the intent of Paul's words for today as, "Do not despise Scripture." The Greek word for "despise" means "to look down upon, to deny, to make or to find contemptible." There are three basic levels of despising God's Word.

Level 1—Despise by not listening, as those with whom God's Spirit did not strive forever; they were judged in the Noahic flood (Gen. 6:3).

Level 2—Despise by listening but not believing, as Judas who betrayed Christ or the followers of Christ who withdrew because of difficult statements (John 6:60, 66).

Level 3—Despise by listening, believing but not obeying, as illustrated by Peter in his three denials (Matt. 26:69-75) or Demas in his desertion of Paul (2 Tim. 4:10).

To avoid any hint of despising Scripture, we need to do three things: listen to understand; believe by faith; and obey to glorify God.

Hold All Things Up to the Light of God's Word

But examine everything carefully.

1 Thessalonians 5:21a

This expands on the previous command. It not only includes teaching which can be either true or false, but involves the experiences of life which can be good or evil.

Here, Paul teaches absolutism, not relativism. The standard for testing all things is the Word of God. Everything requires examination or testing.

All Scripture is inspired by God and profitable for teaching, for reproof, for correction, for training in righteousness; that the man of God may be adequate, equipped for every good work.

2 Timothy 3:16-17

Scripture continually bids us to test or to discern:

For false gods	Deuteronomy 13:1-5
For false prophets	Deuteronomy 18:20-22
For distorted truth	Isaiah 8:20; Revelation 22:18-19
For false teachers	1 John 4:1-3

Two historical tests of eternal significance come to mind. Eve tested Satan's words, but unfortunately not against God's words. She compared his words to her own thoughts, and finding them in agreement, she rejected God and fell into sin (Gen. 3:1-6). The human race has lived in sin ever since.

Jesus tested Satan's words too, but against the Word of God.

In each instance, Satan disagreed with God so Jesus reaffirmed God's Word and utterly rejected Satan (Matt. 4:1-11). Thus Christ remained without sin (2 Cor. 5:21; 1 John 2:29; 3:3, 5).

Involve Yourself in Good Things

Hold fast to that which is good.

1 Thessalonians 5:21b

Determine what is good and then grip it firmly—don't let go. Paul prayed this for the Philippians.

And this I pray, that your love may abound still more and more in real knowledge and all discernment, so that you may approve things that are excellent, in order to be sincere and blameless until the day of Christ.

Philippians 1:9-10

Daniel serves as a life study of one who continually sought the most spiritually excellent way.

But Daniel made up his mind that he would not defile himself with the king's choice food or with the wine which he drank; so he sought permission from the commander of the officials that he might not defile himself.

Daniel 1:8

They tried to give Daniel a Babylonian education (1:4), name (1:7), and diet (1:8). He went along with the teaching because he could test it with Scripture and reject that which was a lie. A new name did not change the character of Daniel and besides, he could not stop them from calling him whatever name they wanted.

Why then did he reject the food, which at first glance seems to be insignificant? When Daniel tested the food against Scripture, he decided that the levitical standard declared it unclean (Lev. 11; Deut. 14); also, the food had been offered to idols (Ex. 34:15; Num. 25:1-2; Deut. 32:37-38).

Scripture declared food and drink offered to idols to be evil; therefore, Daniel refused to take hold of that which was not good.

Join Not with Evil

Abstain from every form of evil.

1 Thessalonians 5:22

Paul prohibited involvement or perceived interest in anything that did not test out as good by the guidelines in Scripture. Like Daniel, we too should abstain from that which God declares evil.

If anyone comes to you and does not bring this teaching, do not receive him into your house, and do not give him a greeting; for the one who gives him a greeting participates in his evil deeds.

2 John 10-11

A Final Tip

Your daily life and your church will continuously provide "the workout facility" for your conditioning routine. Like physical exercise, spiritual exercise gives best results when it is a daily part of your routine. The challenge is now yours to grow strong in the things of Christ.

Like a mighty army
Moves the Church of God;
Brothers, we are treading
Where the saints have trod.
We are not divided,
All one body we—
One in hope and doctrine,
One in charity.[1]

11
ONE-ANOTHER DIRECTIVES

Satan loves disturbance and disruption in the church. His strategy of "divide and conquer" works as well today as it did when he first used it on Eve to separate her from God (Gen. 3:1-7).

On the other hand, biblical history sends signals about false unity which is just as dangerous as division. Jehoshaphat paid the price of ecumenism with Ahab (2 Chron. 19:1-2). Christ confronted the ecumenism of churches in Pergamum (Rev. 2:14-15) and Thyatira (Rev. 2:20-24). Ephesus rejected the Nicolaitans and received the Savior's "Well done!" (Rev. 2:6) Jude encouraged Christians to contend earnestly for the faith (Jude 3).

Unity that pleases God and advances His kingdom will not be at the expense of His Word or character. Unity at the expense of God's Word or character is not true or holy. The oneness Jesus prayed for in John 17 will not compromise truth and righteousness.

Paul's charge to oneness (Phil. 2:1-4) did not countermand his high view of and total commitment to Scripture. The clarion call to one Lord, one faith, and one baptism sounded forth from the same apostle who wrote that all Scripture comes from God; it serves therefore as the measure by which true Christians can discern if a beckon to unity is really of God (Eph. 4:5; 2 Tim. 3:16-17).

The ideals of many ecumenists are peace and love. To interpret this approach accurately, believers must view these commendable qualities through the context of truth. True peace cannot be experienced apart from God's truth (Jer. 33:6; Zech. 8:19); neither can true love (Eph. 4:15; 1 John 3:18).

A major mark of spiritual maturity is to promote unity without compromising truth and righteousness or sacrificing relationships. The alert Christian will be watching for potential disruption and be prepared to biblically deal with it.

Blessed are the peacemakers for they shall be called sons of God.

Matthew 5:9

The Bible on Unity
The Jews sang Psalms 120–134 when ascending to Jerusalem for worship; one of them focused on unity.

Behold, how good and how pleasant it is
For brothers to dwell together in unity!
It is like the precious oil upon the head,
Coming down upon the beard,
Even Aaron's beard,
Coming down upon the edge of his robes.
It is like the dew of Hermon,
Coming down upon the mountains of Zion;
For there the LORD commanded the blessing—
life forever.

Psalm 133

To them, unity appeared as pure as the newly anointed priest (Ex. 29:7; Lev. 8:12). The life-giving water flowing off Mt. Hermon to bring precious water to the rest of Israel pictures the positive dynamic of peace among believers. When the Jew read this psalm, he would likely think of Abraham who said to Lot, "Please let there be no strife between you and me . . . for we are brothers" (Gen. 13:8).

Our Lord Jesus Christ indicated His concern for unity among the disciples. During His last time with them before the cross, He prayed,

And I am no more in the world; and yet they themselves are in the world, and I come to Thee. Holy Father, keep them in Thy name, the name which Thou hast given Me, that they may be one, even as We are.

John 17:11

I do not ask in behalf of these alone, but for those also who believe in Me through their word; that they may all be one; even as Thou, Father, art in Me, and I in Thee, that they also may be in Us; that the world may believe that Thou didst send Me. And the glory which Thou hast given Me I have given to them; that they may be one, just as We are one.

John 17:20-22

His prayer focused on the disciples (17:11), but it also extended to all who would believe in the future—including us (17:20). Christ clearly wants believers to be promoting oneness among the family of God.

The answer to Christ's prayer stands out prominently in the Acts narrative about life in the new church at Jerusalem. On at least five occasions, their unity is highlighted.

One mind in prayer	Acts 1:14
One mind in worship	Acts 2:46
One accord in prayer	Acts 4:24
One heart and soul in sharing their possessions	Acts 4:32

One accord in Christ   Acts 5:12

Paul portrayed oneness in the body of Christ beautifully to the Romans (15:5-6).

Now may the God who gives perseverance and encouragement grant you to be of the same mind with one another according to Christ Jesus; that with one accord you may with one voice glorify the God and Father of our Lord Jesus Christ.

They were to share the same mind, accord, and voice, and in so doing glorify God. On the other hand, he would quickly confront potential or actual division (Rom. 16:17; 1 Cor. 3:3).

Later on Paul wrote to the Philippians that conduct worthy of the Gospel involved unity of mind and spirit (1:27-30). He added that ultimate joy could be experienced only by believers who found unity in the same mind, the same love, the same spirit, and the same purpose (2:1-2).

The Key to Unity

When the King of kings abandoned His heavenly throne, He had to borrow a place to be born, live in a home not His own, ask for a boat to preach from, and be buried in a tomb on loan. Though He was rich, for our sakes He became poor (2 Cor. 8:9). The Apostle Paul explained such radical behavior in Philippians 2:5-8:

Have this attitude in yourselves which was also in Christ Jesus, who, although He existed in the form of God, did not regard equality with God a thing to be grasped, but emptied Himself, taking the form of a bondservant, and being made in the likeness of men. And being found in appearance as a man, He humbled Himself by becoming obedient to the point of death, even death on a cross.

With unmistakable authority, Paul commanded believers to think about one another as Christ thought about them. This idea first entered the discussion in verse 2: "Make my joy complete by being of the same mind . . . united in spirit, intent on one purpose." With humility, they were each "to regard one another as more important than himself." These thoughts precede his explanation for Christ's departure from the presence of God. Christ left heaven:

To seek and save the lost	Luke 19:10
To reveal God	John 1:18
To provide eternal life	John 10:10
To experience human life	Hebrews 2:17-18
To destroy the work of Satan	1 John 3:8

In Philippians 2:5ff, Paul added another reason—to model the mind-set that God demands Christians possess and practice.

Attitudes result in actions. Christ's attitude of sacrifice led Him first to make Himself as nothing; then the attitude of submission caused Him to humble Himself on the cross—all of this to voluntarily fulfill the role of a servant. He served God by accomplishing His salvation purposes (Isa. 42:1; 53:11), and He served us by giving Himself a ransom for many (Matt. 20:28).

The great doctrine known as the "kenosis" emerges from Paul's literary and theological masterpiece. Christ emptied Himself not of His deity, to be sure, but rather of the independent exercise of His divine attributes. He "stripped Himself of the insignia of majesty" and then added to Himself both the internal and external reality of humanity. He took "the form of a bondservant" and was "made in the likeness of men." Servant thinking drove Christ to appear in a body as the God-man—one person both fully God and fully human.

Paul later commented on the Incarnation, "Beyond all question, the mystery of godliness is great" (1 Tim. 3:16, NIV). While all this rich theology and depth of thought eludes our full mental grasp, Paul simply believed that as Christ served so should Christians, for we are to think and then act like Christ (Phil. 2:3-4). D.L. Moody said, "The measure of a man is not how many servants he has, but how many men he serves."

The attitude of sacrifice says, "I am willing, like Christ, to give up my present God-given privileges to follow God's servant-direction for my life." The attitude of submission says, "I am willing, like Christ, to obey God's servant-will for my life even when it involves humiliating life circumstances." This kind of thinking drove Christ to act. Thus He:

- Sacrificed His royal residency in heaven for the slums of this earth (John 6:51).
- Sacrificed His intimate fellowship with holy God to walk among sinful people (John 1:1, 14).
- Sacrificed comforts and pleasures for the pain of an imperfect world (Matt. 27:46).
- Sacrificed His role as sovereign of the universe to be a servant of mankind (Matt. 20:28).
- Lowered His quality of life from peace to war (Matt. 10:34; 1 John 3:8).
- Lowered His environment from purity to sin-bearing (1 Peter 2:24).
- Lowered His lifestyle from riches to poverty (2 Cor. 8:9).
- Lowered His ministry from independence to dependence (John 5:30; 8:28; 12:49).
- Lowered His experience from glory and life to shame and death (John 17:5).

Christian thinking should cause us to give, not get—to let go rather than to grasp selfishly. But the giving up is not without immediate blessing, for Jesus said, "It is more blessed to give than to receive" (Acts 20:35). And don't forget our delayed reward. Concerning Jesus, Paul wrote,

Therefore also God highly exalted Him, and bestowed on Him the name which is above every name, that at the name of Jesus every knee should bow, of those who are in heaven, and on earth, and under the earth, and that every tongue should confess that Jesus Christ is Lord, to the glory of God the Father.

Philippians 2:9-11

God honored Christ's servant role, and attitude of sacrifice

137

and submission, with exaltation. In similar ways, God will exalt the Christian who consistently models Christ's behavior.

> *The greatest among you shall be your servant. And whoever exalts himself shall be humbled; and whoever humbles himself shall be exalted.*
>
> *Matthew 23:11-12*

> *Humble yourselves, therefore, under the mighty hand of God, that He may exalt you at the proper time.*
>
> *1 Peter 5:6*

Our society believes that Christian thinking—servanthood, humility, and submissive obedience—leads to earthly insignificance. But for Jesus and those who follow Him, following the mind of Christ results in eternal impact. So, "Have this attitude in yourselves which was also in Christ Jesus" (Phil. 2:5). As Christ has responded to us, Christians are to act toward one another.

Promoting Unity

> *For just as we have many members in one body and all the members do not have the same function, so we, who are many, are one body in Christ, and individually members one of another.*
>
> *Romans 12:4-5*

> *For the body is not one member, but many.*
>
> *1 Corinthians 12:14*

First, the *principle*. None of us can exist fruitfully and peacefully by ourselves. We belong to a spiritual body of many parts which God intended to work together. Just as an athletic team must work in unison, the parts of a jet airplane operate as one, or the voices of a choir blend in harmony, so the members of Christ's body need to each contribute their part and receive the needed contribution of others.

Oftentimes we think of *functional* unity in terms of each person exercising a spiritual gift (1 Cor. 12:4-11). However, a more foundational unity is called for by the "body principle." We can call it *relational* unity. It's built around the myriad of New Testament exhortations regarding "one another."

Second, the *practice.* Family behavior in the body of Christ all starts with "Love one another." Our Lord told the disciples,

> *By this all men will know that you are My disciples, if you have love for one another.*
>
> *John 13:35*

The epistles refer to this overarching principle at least ten times (Rom. 13:8; 1 Thes. 3:12; 4:9; 2 Thes. 1:3; 1 Peter 1:22; 1 John 3:11, 23; 4:7, 11; 2 John 5).

From this broad statement, the epistles then move to explain the various features of unity active in the church. They are numerous and in general are self-explanatory. So let me list them for you and ask that you slow down here to look up all the passages.

Be devoted	Romans 12:10
Honor by giving preference	Romans 12:10
Be of the same mind	Romans 12:16; 15:5
Build up	Romans 14:19; 1 Thessalonians 5:11
Be at peace	Romans 14:19
Receive/accept	Romans 15:7
Admonish/comfort	Romans 15:14; 1 Thessalonians 4:18; 5:11
Greet	Romans 16:16; 1 Corinthians 16:20; 2 Corinthians 13:12; 1 Peter 5:14
Care	1 Corinthians 12:25
Serve	Galatians 5:13

Bear burdens	Galatians 6:2
Forbear, be patient	Ephesians 4:2; Colossians 3:13
Be kind	Ephesians 4:32
Submit	Ephesians 5:21
Esteem highly	Philippians 2:3
Forgive	Colossians 3:13
Seek the good	1 Thessalonians 5:15
Stimulate	Hebrews 10:24
Confess sins	James 5:16
Pray for	James 5:16
Be hospitable	1 Peter 4:9
Be humble	1 Peter 5:5
Fellowship in the light	1 John 1:7

While total unity is *doctrinal, functional,* and *relational,* when problems exist, we look first at the relational element.

Preventing Disruption

Not only are we to add positive responses to our lifestyle, but we need to eliminate or avoid other responses which Scripture prohibits. Take a careful look at the "do not" side of the "one anothers."

Owe anything but love	Romans 13:8
Judge	Romans 14:13
Defraud/deprive in marriage	1 Corinthians 7:5
Devour/consume	Galatians 5:15
Provoke/challenge	Galatians 5:26
Envy	Galatians 5:26
Lie	Colossians 3:9
Hate	Titus 3:3
Speak against/complain	James 4:11; 5:9

Whether it be a marriage, a family, or the body of Christ, when these mature behavior patterns consistently color life, great harmony and peace will be the experience.

Live in Peace

With the Father called "the God of peace" (2 Cor. 13:11), the Son entitled "the Prince of peace" (Isa. 9:6), and the Spirit producing "the fruit of peace" in believers (Gal. 5:22), it's no wonder then that Paul writes several exhortations to unity.

If possible, so far as it depends on you, be at peace with all men.

Romans 12:18

Live in peace with one another.

1 Thessalonians 5:13b

When peace like a river attendeth my way,
When sorrows like sea billows roll;
Whatever my lot, Thou hast taught me to say,
It is well, it is well with my soul.[1]

12
MEASURING SPIRITUAL MATURITY

Some people calculate their godliness by how well they keep a man-made list of do's and don'ts. That is *legalism.* Those at the other end of the scale determine spirituality by how close they can get to the edge and still not seem to be involved in sin. That is *license.*

Neither way takes God's Word or God's holiness seriously. Both appeal to man's approval or disapproval rather than to God's.

Regardless of what any person thinks, including ourselves, God will one day render His divine analysis about our spirituality. His critique will count for eternity.

Therefore also we have as our ambition, whether at home or absent, to be pleasing to Him. For we must all appear before the judgment seat of Christ, that each one may be recompensed for his deeds in the body, according to what he has done, whether good or bad.

2 Corinthians 5:9-10

Now God has not left us in the dark as to what evidences true spirituality or what we should strive for in our Christian life. Scripture repeatedly outlines the elements of character and lifestyle that God highly values. Paul's words to the Roman Christians lay a foundation.

Therefore do not let what is for you a good thing be spoken of as evil; for the kingdom of God is not eating and drinking, but righteousness and peace and joy in the Holy Spirit. For he who in this way serves Christ is acceptable to God and approved by men.

Romans 14:16-18

This shows us that God is not so much interested in the physical side of life as He is in the spiritual side. Other portions of Scripture more explicitly outline God's spiritual goals for us.

The Call to Measure Our Spirituality

Paul had been arrogantly challenged by the Corinthians to check his own life for proof of Christ's reality (2 Cor. 13:2-3). He countered with this rebuke,

Test yourselves to see if you are in the faith; examine yourselves! Or do you not recognize this about yourselves, that Jesus Christ is in you—unless indeed you fail the test?

2 Corinthians 13:5

That raises the question, "What should they have examined and looked for?" Maybe they thought back to Micah 6:8.

He has told you, O man, what is good; And what does the Lord require of you but to do justice, to love kindness, and to walk humbly with your God?

143

But that's not specific enough. The Apostle John wrote in more detail.

These things I have written to you who believe in the name of the Son of God, in order that you may know that you have eternal life.

1 John 5:13

By what characteristics would his readers know that they possessed eternal life? John listed three broad criteria. The entire book is based on these tests. Here is a brief summary.

● The Test of Obedience. (1:5–2:6; 2:29–3:10)

And by this we know that we have come to know Him, if we keep His commandments.

1 John 2:3

● The Test of Love. (2:7-11; 3:11-24; 4:7–5:5)

We know that we have passed out of death into life, because we love the brethren. He who does not love abides in death.

1 John 3:14

● The Test of Truth about Jesus Christ. (2:18-28; 4:1-6; 5:6-12)

We are from God; he who knows God listens to us; he who is not from God does not listen to us. By this we know the spirit of truth and the spirit of error.

1 John 4:6

Standards of Spirituality

While these statements are helpful for most of us, they still do not give enough details. So we ask for more.

I want to introduce the chief passages in Scripture which provide additional details. In some sense, they serve as spiritual dimensions which we need to measure daily. They involve both positive and negative qualities.

● According to Moses. For most, this would be the first standard. Just remember that since it was first written, the heart or spirit of the fourth commandment, about the Sabbath, has moved from the seventh day to the first day of the week in celebration of Christ's resurrection (1 Cor. 16:1; Rev. 1:10; Col. 2:16).

Then God spoke all these words, saying, "I am the LORD your God, who brought you out of the land of Egypt, out of the house of slavery.

1. You shall have no other gods before Me.

2. You shall not make for yourself an idol, or any likeness of what is in heaven above or on the earth beneath or in the water under the earth. You shall not worship them or serve them. . . .

3. You shall not take the name of the LORD your God in vain, for the Lord will not leave him unpunished who takes His name in vain.

4. Remember the sabbath day, to keep it holy. Six days you shall labor and do all your work, but the seventh day is a sabbath of the Lord your God. . . .

5. Honor your father and your mother, that your days may be prolonged in the land which the Lord your God gives you.

6. You shall not murder.

7. You shall not commit adultery.

8. You shall not steal.

9. You shall not bear false witness against your neighbor.

10. You shall not covet your neighbor's house; you shall not covet your neighbor's wife or his male servant or his female servant or his ox or his donkey or anything that belongs to your neighbor.

Exodus 20:1-17

● According to Jesus.

Blessed are the poor in spirit, for theirs is the kingdom of heaven.

Blessed are those who mourn, for they shall be comforted.
Blessed are the gentle, for they shall inherit the earth.
Blessed are those who hunger and thirst for righteousness,
for they shall be satisfied.
Blessed are the merciful, for they shall receive mercy.
Blessed are the pure in heart, for they shall see God.
Blessed are the peacemakers, for they shall be called sons of
God.
Blessed are those who have been persecuted for the sake of
righteousness, for theirs is the kingdom of heaven.
Blessed are you when men cast insults at you, and perse-
cute you, and say all kinds of evil against you falsely, on
account of Me.
Rejoice, and be glad for your reward in heaven is great, for
so they persecuted the prophets who were before you.
Matthew 5:3-12

● According to Paul.

The fruit of the Spirit is love, joy, peace, patience, kind-
ness, goodness, faithfulness, gentleness, self-control;
against such things there is no law.
Galatians 5:22-23

Love is patient, love is kind, and is not jealous; love does
not brag and is not arrogant, does not act unbecomingly; it
does not seek its own, is not provoked, does not take into
account wrong suffered, does not rejoice in unrighteous-
ness, but rejoices with the truth; bears all things, believes
all things, hopes all things, endures all things.
1 Corinthians 13:4-7

● According to Peter.

Applying all diligence, in your faith supply moral excel-
lence, and in your moral excellence, knowledge; and in
your knowledge, self-control, and in your self-control, per-
severance, and in your perseverance, godliness; and in

*your godliness, brotherly kindness, and in your brotherly
kindness, love. For if these qualities are yours and are
increasing, they render you neither useless nor unfruitful
in the true knowledge of our Lord Jesus Christ.*

2 Peter 1:5-8

Remember! Each writer exhorted the believers to live with
greater consistency each day and to make these qualities
their pattern of living. The Bible does not teach "perfection-
ism" as a goal or hope in this life. Never does Scripture
demand or expect a continuous, sinless experience. That's
why God has made provision for believers to be cleansed of
the immediate filth of sin (James 5:16; 1 John 2:1-2).

What is your response? If you say, "Forget it! These are
irrelevant, plus they are too difficult. No one can do that!"
you need to examine yourself, as Paul told the Corinthians.
People who want a form of godliness without the Spirit's
power to transform their lives have not really embraced
Christ (2 Tim. 3:2-5). They are the shallow soil or the weed-
infested soil, as in Jesus' parable of the four soils (Matt. 13:5-
7, 20-22).

You might be saying, "That's the deep desire of my heart!
I know that's right and I want to make godliness a greater
part of my life and a more consistent pattern of my Christian
walk." That is the expected response of a true believer and
one in whom the Spirit lives and works.

On the other hand, we should be so consumed by what we
have just read that not one of us should ask, "Since I'm doing
so well, is there more?" But for the sake of being true to
Scripture, let me show you the ultimate. Without this final
quality, our quest for godliness would remain incomplete.

The Final Standard—Contentment

Phillip Keller, keenly aware of what true spirituality involves,
notes, "Contentment should be the hallmark of the man or
woman who has put his or her affairs in the hands of God."[2]

Paul outlines four elements which build spiritual contentment in the believer, as a conclusion to his letter to the Philippians. In an era of materialistic selfishness, nothing could be more appropriate for a Christian to understand and implement. It crowns the head of spiritual maturity.

● Element One—Confidence in God's Power.

But I rejoiced in the Lord greatly, that now at last you have revived your concern for me; indeed, you were concerned before, but you lacked opportunity. Not that I speak from want; for I have learned to be content in whatever circumstances I am. I know how to get along with humble means, and I also know how to live in prosperity; in any and every circumstance I have learned the secret of being filled and going hungry, both of having abundance and suffering need. I can do all things through Him who strengthens me.
Philippians 4:10-13

Paul spoke from the crucible of his own life, outlining the basic truths which flow out of a firm belief in God's sovereign and all-powerful control of this world and our lives.

Contentment looks first to God (4:10).
Contentment can be learned (4:11-12).
Contentment does not depend on life circumstances (4:11-12).
Contentment is not based on self-sufficiency (4:13).
Contentment finds its source in Christ's strength (4:13).

● Element Two—Confidence in God's Providence.

Nevertheless, you have done well to share with me in my affliction. . . . Not that I seek the gift itself, but I seek for the profit which increases to your account. But I have received everything in full, and have an abundance; I am amply supplied, having received from Epaphroditus what you have sent, a fragrant aroma, an acceptable sacrifice, well-pleasing to God.
Philippians 4:14-18

Paul didn't encourage the Philippians to look for the miraculous, such as God's care for the Israelites in the wilderness (Deut. 8:3-4). Rather, he explained how God had provided for him through their gifts.

● Element Three—Confidence in God's Promises.

And my God shall supply all your needs according to His riches in glory in Christ Jesus.

Philippians 4:19

This certainly stands as one of the great promises of Scripture. Christians in other times and different places have appreciated and experienced it even more vividly than we do today. Paul encouraged them that God would meet their needs just as they had met his. It is a companion to other great texts on God's promises such as,

Blessed be the Lord, who has given rest to His people Israel, according to all that He promised; not one word has failed of all His good promise, which He promised through Moses His servant.

1 Kings 8:56

For as many as may be the promises of God, in Him they are yes; wherefore also by Him is our Amen to the glory of God through us.

2 Corinthians 1:20

For by these He has granted to us His precious and magnificent promises, in order that by them you might become partakers of the divine nature, having escaped the corruption that is in the world by lust.

2 Peter 1:4

● Element Four—Confidence in God's Eternal Purposes.

Now to our God and Father be the glory forever and ever. Amen.

Philippians 4:20

*So David blessed the Lord in the sight of all the assembly;
and David said, "Blessed art Thou, O Lord God of Israel
our father, forever and ever. Thine, O Lord, is the greatness and the power and the glory and the victory and the
majesty, indeed everything that is in the heavens and the
earth; Thine is the dominion, O Lord, and Thou dost exalt
Thyself as head over all. Both riches and honor come from
Thee, and Thou dost rule over all, and in Thy hand is
power and might; and it lies in Thy hand to make great,
and to strengthen everyone. Now therefore, our God, we
thank Thee, and praise Thy glorious name."*

1 Chronicles 29:10-13

Contentment then is a satisfied spiritual view of life that
yields all personal rights to the higher purposes of God's will
and glory. It also has the ultimate confidence in God to sustain and strengthen, regardless of what life brings. It's not a
stoic self-suffering, but is a spiritual God-dependency.

Now why is this the final standard? Listen to Paul!

*But godliness actually is a means of great gain, when
accompanied by contentment. For we have brought nothing
into the world, so we cannot take anything out of it either.
And if we have food and covering, with these we shall be
content.*

1 Timothy 6:6-8

Unless contentment completes our godliness, then we fall
short of the spiritual goal. If we want to be godly, then we
must also be confident that He will take care of us. With that
comes contentment.

Pressing On

In this chapter I have given you some of the key Scriptures
by which we can measure our spirituality as God measures it.
No one will ever fully become all that the New Testament
exhorts us to be. Yet, we are to continue toward full maturity.
Paul puts it all in proper perspective for the Philippians. So,

we let him have the last word in our discussion.

Not that I have already obtained it, or have already become perfect, but I press on in order that I may lay hold of that for which also I was laid hold of by Christ Jesus. Brethren, I do not regard myself as having laid hold of it yet; but one thing I do: forgetting what lies behind and reaching forward to what lies ahead, I press on toward the goal for the prize of the upward call of God in Christ Jesus.

Let us therefore, as many as are perfect, have this attitude; and if in anything you have a different attitude, God will reveal that also to you; however, let us keep living by that same standard to which we have attained.

Philippians 3:12-16

O hope of every contrite heart,
O joy of all the meek,
To those who fall, how kind Thou art!
How good to those who seek![1]

13
WHAT IF I FALL?

Life boils down to one word—WARFARE. Life consists of a daily struggle to meet deadlines, satisfy people, balance the checkbook, mow the lawn, clean the house, avoid mistakes, fight the freeway, earn passing grades, watch the waistline, or just simply keep our heads above water.

Our most formidable foe, Satan, attacks through constant confrontation with sin. The conflict rages without ceasing. For example, David, the God-anointed king of Israel, fought a battle one day with this archenemy and lost. In Psalm 51 we read how he succumbed to the opposition but, nevertheless, won the war. From him we can learn how to overcome sin's damaging blow when it throws an uppercut to the chin of a true believer.

David doesn't stand alone, either. Peter denied Christ three times (Matt. 26:69-75). Moses once failed to treat God in a holy manner (Deut. 32:51). John Mark proved unfaithful in his first major ministry assignment (Acts 13:13; 15:38). The church at Ephesus left its first love (Rev. 2:4). Demas deserted Paul (2 Tim. 4:10). Israel lost favor with God (Rom. 11:11-24). Achan disobeyed (Josh. 7:22-26). Nadab and Abihu profaned the tabernacle service (Lev. 10:1-2). Ananias and Sapphira lied to God (Acts 5:1-11). Uzziah made an unauthorized sacrifice (2 Chron. 26:16-21). Uzzah touched the ark (2 Sam. 6:6-7).

Some died immediately for their transgressions; others lived a while before God's judgment. Still others lived a full life by God's mercy. But none chronicles the details of their sin and God's dealing with them as David did after his transgression with Bathsheba (2 Sam. 11–12). David's diary presents his spiritual spill and subsequent recovery in order to assist others who have gravely sinned but whom God has sovereignly and mercifully let live. Psalm 51 answers the question, "What if this happens to me?"

David's Situation

David was not a "one-woman man"; 2 Samuel 3:1-5 names six of his wives. Because Jerusalem lived in peace and the tabernacle resided on God's mountain, David's attentions turned from God's agenda to more women. While his troops were out securing the kingdom, their king stayed at home and attempted to conquer a woman's heart (2 Sam. 11:1-5).

In so doing, he directly violated the last five of the Ten Commandments—four of the five demanding the death penalty (Ex. 20:13-17). David murdered, committed adultery, stole Bathsheba's heart from her husband, gave false witness against Uriah, and coveted his neighbor's wife.

In fact, David had also dishonored his parents, profaned the Sabbath with unholy worship, taken God's sacred name in vain, made women his idol and disobediently viewed them as idolatrous objects of worship. David represents the classic case of breaking the law in one point and thus violating it in all points (James 2:10). No wonder the divine commentary on David's escapade reads, "But the thing that David had done was evil in the sight of the Lord" (2 Sam. 11:27).

Second Samuel 12:1-23 and Psalm 32 detail David's initial denial and his later confession of sin. He suffered greatly before he admitted his sins to Nathan; and even with this, his life would be plagued to the end by tragedies in his own household, by the enemies of the Lord having occasion to blaspheme God because of his sin, and by the death of Bathsheba's child (12:11-14). But the Lord mercifully took away David's sin and let him live (12:13).

Psalm 51 outlines the steps of spiritual rehabilitation that David took in the midst of an apparently hopeless situation. First, he confessed his sin before God—open repentance (51:1-6). Second, David prayed for God's restoration (51:7-12). Finally, the king of Israel recommitted himself and prayed that God would use him as before (51:13-19). If you are now facing similar circumstances, then David's response to God needs to be your course of action.

David's Repentance
David's testimony illustrates eight characteristics that distinguish between true repentance like David's and the selfish regret that Judas displayed (Matt. 27:3). You can measure your own honesty and genuineness by comparing them to David's account (51:1-6).

• David openly admitted his sin when confronted by a godly man (2 Sam. 12:13). He didn't lie about it, deny it, make excuses, bargain, minimize the sin, deflect the conversation to the sin of others, talk about extenuating circumstances, seek to explain it from his childhood, blame his weaknesses, call sin a sickness, or attempt to justify what he had done. He forthrightly announced, "I have sinned against the Lord." He courageously owned up to his transgressions.

• David's guilt drove him to cry out for God's mercy, grace, and cleansing (Ps. 51:1-2). Nathan stalked David on the outside and guilt pursued him on the inside—both God's spiritual agents. The physical and emotional wounds of sin drove David to despair before he asked for God's healing hand (Ps. 32:3-5). He appealed to God's compassionate character (Ex.

34:6), asking God to use a spiritual peroxide and clean out his sinful wound. He could not live with the pain of unresolved sin any longer.

• David openly acknowledged his unrighteous disposition (Ps. 51:3-5). David affirmed what God knew all along—his sins and transgressions. In a day when the Christian community seems to minimize or explain away sin, a fresh dose of David's honesty is greatly needed (see 1 Kings 8:46; 2 Chron. 6:36; Pss. 130:3-4; 143:2; Rom. 3:23). He did not excuse his behavior on the grounds of psychological predisposition, childhood traumas, or sexual addiction. Rather, he took the personal responsibility for his own sin.

• David understood that the ultimate issue involved is sin (Ps. 51:4a). There is no sin that is not first against God who is holy (Isa. 6:3). That's why Joseph, when confronted by the sexual lure of Potiphar's wife, cried out, "How then could I do this great evil and sin against God?" (Gen. 39:9) Until this level of understanding sin can be acknowledged, true repentance has not been genuinely manifested.

• David submitted to God's standards of moral right and wrong (Ps. 51:4b). "And done what is evil in Thy sight." David did not judge his actions from the perspective of societal norms, government standards, the legal, educational, or religious communities, the moralists of his day, or even his own values. He allowed God to determine what constituted righteous or unrighteous behavior (Pss. 19:8; 33:4). God's Word stood as the ultimate authority in David's experience.

• David willingly accepted whatever punishment God deemed just (Ps. 51:4c). When Nathan told David of the rich man wronging the poor shepherd (2 Sam. 12:1-4), David sentenced the rich man to die; and in that case, it only involved the rich stealing from the poor. When David realized that he was the man, it is no wonder that he cried out with a truly repentant spirit, "Thou art justified when Thou dost speak, and blameless when Thou dost judge." He had, in fact, broken all Ten Commandments, and anything less than death would be unimaginable and a superlative extension of mercy.

• David reenrolled in the school of truth (Ps. 51:6). I think it is safe to say that if David had been faithful to the classroom of God's Word all along, he never would have misused his idle time to get involved with Bathsheba (Ps. 119:9-11). He had been absent too long from a daily diet of truth; here he expressed his hunger for truth and wisdom.

● David publicly shared his brutal battle with sin to warn others who might otherwise walk in the same sinful way (Ps. 32:5). When Jesus warned Peter that Satan would sift him, He concluded, "When you return, strengthen your brothers" (Luke 22:32). David demonstrated in his confession a deep desire to direct others away from sin, even at the expense of his own humiliation. For thousands of years, David's autobiographical account has been available in Scripture for all to read.

Search me, O God, and know my heart;
Try me and know my anxious thoughts;
And see if there be any hurtful way in me,
And lead me in the everlasting way.
Psalm 139:23-24

David's Prayer for God's Restoration
In Revelation 2:4-5, the Lord of the church confronted the Ephesian church over leaving their first love and abandoning their beginning works. He gave them three steps to follow if they wanted to continue enjoying God's blessing:
Remember back to your first love and beginning works.
Repent of your present sin.
Return to your roots of love and good deeds.
The alternative was not pleasant. ". . . or else I am coming to you, and will remove your lampstand out of its place—unless you repent" (2:5). Jesus could not have been clearer—repent and I will continue in your presence. *Or,* continue to sin and I will remove your ministry.

This pattern for Ephesus repeats the pattern of David established 1,000 years earlier. Because of its timeless nature, the same process is also in place today. David prayed in Psalm 51:7-12 that God would restore to him the blessings (not the reality) of his salvation which were forfeited during his spree of unconfessed sin. It is amazing how much David gave up, in light of how little he had to gain by his sin.

● Personal Holiness (Ps. 51:7, 9b-10a). "Purify me with hyssop, and I shall be clean; wash me, and I shall be whiter than snow . . . and blot out all my iniquities. Create in me a clean heart, O God. . . . " David came to the right Person — for only God can forgive sin. When He does, we are made white as snow, even though our sin be like scarlet (Isa. 1:18). He removes sin as far as the east from the west (Ps. 103:12). Our forgiven sin is cast into the depth of the sea (Micah 7:19). God casts our sin behind His back where He will never see it again (Isa. 38:17). David was dirty with sin, and so he asked God to cleanse him.

● Emotional Peace (Ps. 51:8a). "Make me to hear joy and gladness." Both of these internal instruments had been silenced by sin and David agonizingly desired their return. God graciously responded and David declared in a burst of testimony and exhortation,

Be glad in the Lord and rejoice you righteous ones, and shout for joy all you who are upright in heart.
Psalm 32:11

● Physical Health (Ps. 51:8b). "Let the bones which Thou hast broken rejoice." His physical pain was as intense as if David had multiple fractures. He described it in Psalm 32:3-4 as his body wasting away, groaning throughout the day, and losing his energy as with the intense heat of summer. It seems that David experienced what doctors call "emotionally induced illness." The heaviness of guilt took a major toll on his physical well-being.

● Intimacy with God (Ps. 51:9a). "Hide Thy face from my sins." David was ashamed of his sin and did not want God to look on him in that state. Perhaps David had in mind the words he had written earlier.

The eyes of the Lord are toward the righteous, and His

157

ears are open to their cry. The face of the Lord is against evildoers, to cut off the memory of them from the earth.
Psalm 34:15-16

● Spiritual Integrity (Ps. 51:10b). "Renew a steadfast heart in me." In sin, David lost his loyalty, faithfulness, and dependability. What he once was known for, sin had destroyed. Most of all, David had violated God's trust. Now with his sin behind both him and God, he turned again to his Lord to seek provision of what he had lost.

● Assurance (Ps. 51:11a). "Do not cast me away from Thy presence." David was not pleading for his salvation, but that he might once again resume his usefulness to the Lord. Paul wrote of such things, discussing how he had with meticulous discipline conducted his life according to God's standard lest he be disqualified (1 Cor. 9:24-27).

● Spiritual Power (Ps. 51:11b). "And do not take Thy Holy Spirit from me." David was referring here to the Holy Spirit's presence for empowerment in the kingship. David knew full well what happened to Saul when he sinned—the Spirit departed. He knew that God would be equally just to remove the Spirit's power which had been given at his own anointing to the kingship of Israel (see 1 Sam. 16:13-14).

● The Joy of Salvation (Ps. 51:12a). The norm had already been expressed by David (Ps. 13:5-6).

But I have trusted in Thy lovingkindness; my heart shall rejoice in Thy salvation. I will sing to the Lord, because He has dealt bountifully with me.

David had forfeited the joy of salvation, and he could not sing of his redemption as he once had.

● Sustaining Grace (Ps. 51:12b). David was totally uncertain of his future as he cried out. He had done the only reasonable thing—thrown himself on the mercy of the court (51:4). Remembering that God withdrew His graces from Saul, David prayed in fear and trust combined.

The radical route of spiritual recovery which David took

involved not only total repentance, but also an earnest, prayerful plea for God to bring a revival of what had once been experienced but was now overshadowed by sin.

David's Recommitment

With repentance and revival behind him, the king now recommitted himself to some basics that once characterized his life but had been absent for a season of sin. In the final seven verses of Psalm 51, David focused on the spiritual priorities of personal testimony (v. 13); song of salvation (v. 14); praises to the Savior (v. 15); true worship (vv. 16-17); prayer for Israel (vv. 18-19).

There can be no doubt that God sovereignly used David's experience to warn us. The price and pain of sin are too great. For those who miss this divine CAUTION and sin, it's God's word of hope. As David found personal restoration in his redemptive relationship with God, so can those who have tragically followed him in sin, if they are willing also to find their way out through repentance.

God's Reaffirmation of David

Did God accept David's repentance as genuine? Did God answer David's revived plea for restoration? Did God respond to David's prayer of recommitment? Listen carefully to God's affirmation, "I have found David the son of Jesse, a man after my own heart, who will do all my will" (Acts 13:22). Since these words were penned a millennium after David's sin, we can assume that God brought recovery to David's life. You can read of these events in David's life in 2 Samuel 12– 1 Kings 2.

No sin is so great that God cannot forgive it. But it must be dealt with on God's terms according to God's will. In all cases God's terms begin with true repentance. In David's case, God's will involved restoration.

Were the whole realm of nature mine,
That were a present far too small;
Love so amazing, so divine,
Demands my soul, my life, my all.[1]

POSTSCRIPT

No spiritual shepherd worthy of his charge would dare lead the flock without first praying for them. When he prays, he acknowledges Christ as the Chief Shepherd (1 Peter 5:4) and invokes God's strength to accomplish His purposes in the church. Remember, Epaphras prayed that the Colossians would "stand firm in all the will of God, mature and fully assured" (Col. 4:12, NIV).

I do not want to close without expressing my heart to pray for you. If you're curious to know how I should pray, look at Paul's petitions on behalf of Christians in his day. They are my models.

I pray that the eyes of your heart may be enlightened, that you may know what is the hope of His calling, what are the riches of the glory of His inheritance in the saints, and

*what is the surpassing greatness of His power toward us
who believe. These are in accordance with the working of
the strength of His might.*

Ephesians 1:18-19

*For this reason, I bow my knees before the Father . . . so
that Christ may dwell in your hearts through faith, and
that you, being rooted and grounded in love, may be able to
comprehend with all the saints what is the breadth and
length and height and depth, and to know the love of Christ
which surpasses knowledge, that you may be filled up to all
the fulness of God.*

Ephesians 3:14, 17-19

*And this I pray, that your love may abound still more and
more in real knowledge and all discernment, so that you
may approve the things that are excellent.*

Philippians 1:9-10

*We have not ceased to pray for you that you may walk in a
manner worthy of the Lord, to please Him in all respects,
bearing fruit in every good work and increasing in the
knowledge of God.*

Colossians 1:9-10

According to the pattern of Paul's prayers, the highest priority in your Christianity will be to cultivate a growing likeness to God in character and conduct by submitting to the
transforming power of God's Word and God's Spirit.

As spiritual maturity becomes your experience, these wonderful words will more frequently be on your lips.

*I'll love Thee in life,
I will love Thee in death,
And praise Thee as long
As Thou lendest me breath;
And say when the death-dew
Lies cold on my brow;
If ever I loved Thee,
My Jesus, 'tis now.*[2]

PERSONAL AND GROUP STUDY GUIDE

Before beginning your personal or group study of *Spiritual Maturity*, take time to read these introductory comments.

If you are working through the study on your own, you may want to adapt certain sections (for example, the icebreakers), and record your responses to all questions in a separate notebook. You might find it more enriching or motivating to study with a partner with whom you can share answers or insights.

If you are leading a group, you may want to ask your group members to read each assigned chapter and work through the study questions before the group meets. This isn't always easy for busy adults, so encourage them with occasional phone calls or notes between meetings. Help members manage their time by pointing out how they can cover a few pages each day. Also have them identify a regular time of the day or week that they can devote to the study. They too may write their responses to the questions in notebooks.

Notice that each session includes the following features:

Session Topic—a brief statement summarizing the session.
Icebreaker—an activity to help group members get better acquainted with the session topic and/or with each other.
Group Discovery Questions—a list of questions to encourage individual discovery or group participation.
Personal Application Questions—an aid to applying the knowledge gained through study to one's personal living. (Note: These are important questions for group members to answer for themselves, even if they do not wish to discuss their responses in the meeting.)

Optional Activities — supplemental ideas that will enhance the study.

Prayer Focus — suggestions for turning one's learning into prayer.

Assignment — activities or preparation to complete prior to the next session.

Here are a few tips which can help you more effectively lead small group studies:

Pray for each group member, asking the Lord to help you create an open atmosphere where everyone will feel free to share with one another and you.

Encourage group members to bring their Bibles as well as their texts to each session. This study guide is based on the *New International Version*, but it is good to have several translations on hand for purposes of comparison.

Start and end on time. This is especially important for the first meeting because it will set the pattern for the rest of the sessions.

Begin with prayer, asking the Holy Spirit to open hearts and minds and to give understanding so that truth will be applied.

Involve everyone. As learners, we retain only 10% of what we hear; 20% of what we see; 65% of what we hear and see; but 90% of what we hear, see, and do.

Promote a relaxed environment. Arrange the chairs in a circle or semicircle. This allows eye contact among members and encourages dynamic discussion. Be relaxed in your own attitude and manner. Be willing to share yourself.

1
THE FIRST STEP

Session Topic: God initiates and sustains our salvation, the starting point for spiritual maturity.

Icebreakers *(Choose one)*
1. Briefly share your salvation testimony. If your group is large, do so in groups of four to six.
2. Some people who come to know the Lord as children think they have boring testimonies in comparison to others who were great sinners before they repented. Is this true? Why or why not?

Group Discovery Questions
1. Why do we need to focus on spiritual infancy before studying spiritual maturity?
2. Read Mark 10:17-22. How did the rich young ruler define salvation? Look at the list of commandments in Exodus 20:3-17. Which ones wasn't he keeping? What do they focus on? Why did Jesus tell him to "sell everything you have and give to the poor, and you will have treasure in heaven. Then come, follow me"?
3. Read Luke 18:13-14. How did this man define salvation? How does his approach differ from the rich young ruler's?
4. Read the accounts of Paul's salvation in Acts 9:1-9; 22:1-11; 26:1-20; and Philippians 3:1-11. Summarize his salvation testimony. How did he define salvation?
5. How would you explain salvation to someone who has never heard the biblical teaching?
6. What is God's role in salvation? What is man's responsibility? What is Christ's role? What is the Holy Spirit's role?
7. What changes should we expect to see in someone who puts his or her faith in Christ for salvation from sin?

Personal Application Questions
1. What evidence in your life indicates you are a Christian?

2. Look again at the textbook list of sins and stumbling-blocks believers are to put off. Which ones do you need to get rid of?

3. Choose one sin you need to put off. What will you do this week to get rid of it?

4. Review the list in the text of actions and character qualities believers are to put on. Which ones do you most need to incorporate into your life? What will you do this week to make it a part of your lifestyle?

Optional Activities

1. Ask four to six Christians at various stages of spiritual growth to define spirituality. Compare their definitions with the one the author gives in the introduction.

2. Write out your salvation testimony, including what you were like before you were saved and some of the differences God has made since that time. Rework it until you can tell it clearly without a lot of Christian buzz words in five to ten minutes.

3. Ask two or three unsaved people how to become God's child. After they answer, ask for their permission to share the biblical answer and/or your testimony.

Prayer Focus

Thank God for the salvation He has provided through Christ's death and for the power of the Holy Spirit to change us. Ask for His help to put off sins and to put on godly character qualities.

Assignment

1. Pray that God will give you at least one opportunity to share your testimony and/or the plan of salvation this week.

2. Read chapter 2 of the text, and identify characteristics of a growing Christian.

2
GROWING IN GRACE

Session Topic: True salvation results in visible spiritual growth.

Icebreakers *(Choose one)*
1. Discuss: What are the characteristics of a growing baby or child? How do these relate to spiritual growth?
2. Identify a picture, metaphor, or simile of growth in the physical realm. Explain how it is related to growth in the spiritual realm.

Group Discovery Questions
1. Why is there so little emphasis in some Christian groups on spiritual growth after salvation?
2. Why is spiritual growth rooted in holiness—both God's and ours?
3. In your own words, what is sanctification?
4. Read Psalm 1. What does a growing believer not do? Do? What are the results?
5. What are some obstacles to pursuing holiness?
6. Read Ephesians 4:11-16. What process for spiritual growth is taught in this passage? How does it contradict the Lone Ranger philosophy of Christian growth so prevalent in America today?

Personal Application Questions
1. How much is spiritual growth emphasized in your group?
2. How important is spiritual growth to you? What concrete evidence supports your answer?
3. Reread the list of vital signs of a true Christian in the text. Which ones are present in your life? Which ones do you need to ask God to help you cultivate?
4. What one vital sign do you want to begin to develop this week? Write a specific, practical plan for doing so.
5. What is currently hindering your spiritual growth? What

do you need to do to get rid of it?

6. How can you increase your understanding of God's holiness and what He wants to accomplish in you?

7. What are you doing to help another believer grow spiritually? What *can* you do?

Optional Activities

1. Do a word study of *holy/holiness* in Scripture. Summarize your findings as a list, chart, song (new words to a familiar tune), poster, or other expression.

2. Study what God says about spiritual discipline in the following passages: Deuteronomy 8:1-5; Psalm 94:12-15; Proverbs 3:11-12; Matthew 18:15-17; John 15:1-4; 1 Corinthians 5:1-13; 11:27-32; 2 Corinthians 12:7-10; Hebrews 12:4-11; Revelation 3:19-20. What is the most helpful or challenging truth you learned from this study?

Prayer Focus

Thank God for specific ways He has helped you grow spiritually and ask for continued growth. Silently confess any sins that are hindering your growth.

Assignment

1. Locate a copy of *If* by Amy Carmichael (Christian Literature Crusade) and read it this week.

2. Read chapter 3 of the text. Think about how you would describe God to someone who has never heard of Him.

3
WHAT IS GOD LIKE?

Session Topic: Knowing who God is and what He is like motivates us to greater spiritual maturity.

Icebreakers *(Choose one)*
1. Using a 2' length of aluminum foil, tear or sculpt an object that represents one of God's characteristics. Share it with your group members and tell why you chose it.
2. Share: What characteristic of God means the most to you? Why?

Group Discovery Questions
1. Read one of the Psalms listed in the text. (Each group member should read a different one.) How do the psalmists describe God's character and worth? Compile a master list.
2. Jewish people recite the *Shema* (Deut. 6:4-5) to remind them of who God is and to prepare their hearts for worship. Read this confession of faith. What do you learn about God from it?
3. How do God's names help us know Him better?
4. Identify a recent situation in which you experienced one of God's attributes. How did knowing this characteristic help you?
5. Compare Job's (Job 38:1–42:6), Isaiah's (Isaiah 6:1-8), and Habakkuk's (Book of Habakkuk) encounters with God. What did they learn about God? How did they respond to this knowledge?

Personal Application Questions
1. Why is a biblical view of God important to spiritual maturity?
2. Identify one problem/trial you are currently struggling with. Which of God's attributes can help you in it?
3. Which of God's communicable attributes do you need to develop in your life? Which one will you start with?

4. Can you name one attribute of God for each letter of the alphabet?

5. Which of God's names is most meaningful to you? Why?

6. How often do you praise God for who He is? How can you incorporate more praise into your daily schedule?

Optional Activities

1. Look through a hymnbook for songs that focus on who God is and what He is like. Sing a few in praise to God.

2. Read one of the four Gospels, noting what Jesus Christ is like both in character and works.

Prayer Focus

Praise God for His specific attributes and names. If you have time, pray through the alphabet, praising Him for one characteristic for each letter.

Assignment

1. Meditate often on one of God's attributes this week.

2. Praise God for a different attribute or name each day this week.

3. Read chapter 4 of the text. Review your growth in godliness since you became God's child. Try to identify specific people and situations that contributed to significant growth spurts.

4. Read a book on the names of God, such as *My Father's Names* by Elmer L. Towns (Regal), *Names of God* by Nathan Stone (Moody), or *Lord, I Want to Know You* by Kay Arthur (Revell). Share one or two insights with someone from your group.

4
TO BE LIKE GOD!

Session Topic: Godliness begins with consecration to God, yields a character like God's, and results in changed conduct.

Icebreakers *(Choose one)*
1. When someone mentions the word *godliness,* what's the first thing you think of?
2. Find something (other than a Bible) in your wallet, purse, pockets, briefcase, or other bag you have with you that represents an aspect of godliness. For example, a calendar or organizer book represents the fact that you schedule time to be with God in order to get to know Him better. Show your object and tell why you chose it.

Group Discovery Questions
1. In your own words, describe a godly person. What does one look like? How does one act? What does one say? What does one think about?
2. How do consecration, character, and conduct contribute to godliness?
3. Read 2 Peter 1:2-11. According to Peter, how do we become like God? Be specific. Who is responsible for our growth in godliness?
4. What are the initial steps we need to take to develop godliness?
5. Read 2 Samuel 22. How are the three elements of godliness (consecration, character, and conduct) demonstrated in this passage?
6. What is God's role in our pursuit of godliness? What are our responsibilities?

Personal Application Questions
1. Reread the five marks of a godly person in the text. Which ones characterize your life?
2. What are some practical ways you can focus on God to

promote a more godly character?

3. Review your life as a Christian. What roles have consecration, character, and conduct played in your spiritual development?

4. How much have you progressed in godliness in the past six months?

5. How pleased are you with your growth in godliness? If your growth does not meet your expectations, what has been hindering it?

6. What area of godliness would you like to grow in? How will you do so?

Optional Activities

1. Start a journal to record your progress in godliness. Write out your goals, steps to achieve them, successes, defeats, and prayers.

2. Talk to a mature believer who has known the Lord longer than you have. Ask for his or her advice on growing in godliness. Note one concrete suggestion you can practice this week.

Prayer Focus

Ask God to help you grow to become more like Him. Make Richard of Chichester's prayer at the end of the chapter your own.

Assignment

1. Memorize Titus 2:11-14 and live it this week.

2. Read chapter 5 of the text. If you are unsure about the Holy Spirit's work in our lives, read about Him and His work in a Bible dictionary, Bible encyclopedia or theology book, such as *Basic Theology* by Charles C. Ryrie (Victor Books).

5
INVADED BY GOD'S SPIRIT

Session Topic: The Holy Spirit is central to and indispensable in spiritual maturity.

Icebreakers *(Choose one)*
1. Complete this statement: When the Holy Spirit is mentioned, I think of. . . .
2. Twist six chenille wires into a sculpture that represents the Holy Spirit. Show your object and tell how it relates to the Spirit.

Group Discovery Questions
1. How does the Holy Spirit's indwelling contribute to our spiritual maturity?
2. What is Spirit baptism? How is it related to spiritual maturity?
3. How does the sealing of the Holy Spirit contribute to our spiritual maturity?
4. Read Galatians 5:13-26. Describe a person who is not Spirit-controlled and one who is walking in the Spirit.
5. How is the fruit of the Spirit produced? See John 15:1-17.
6. What are spiritual gifts? Compile a list of specific gifts from Romans 12:6-8; 1 Corinthians 12:28-30; Ephesians 4:11; and 1 Peter 4:10-11.
7. What does it mean to be filled with the Spirit? How do we obey this command?

Personal Application Questions
1. How has your concept of the Holy Spirit changed as a result of reading this chapter and participating in this study?
2. Look at Galatians 5:13-26 again. Which deeds of the flesh need to be weeded out of your life? Which fruit of the Spirit need to be developed more?
3. Choose one fruit of the Spirit that is in short supply in your life. What can you do this week to begin to grow more?

4. What spiritual gift(s) did God give you? How are you using it/them?

5. If you do not know what your gift is, what can you do this week to begin to discover it?

6. Are you presently controlled by the Holy Spirit? How do you know?

7. What keeps you from being filled or controlled by the Spirit?

Optional Activities

1. Do a study on the fruit of the Spirit. An inductive Bible study guide, such as *The Growing Season* by Lin Johnson (Victor Books), can give you direction and help.

2. Draw a large circle on a sheet of paper, and divide it into eight pie-shaped wedges. Label each a different area of your life, such as family, recreation, thoughts, time, friends, money, work, and goals. Shade each area to represent the amount of it you have yielded to the Holy Spirit's control. What does your shading reveal about the Spirit's control of your life?

Prayer Focus

Thank God for the indwelling, baptism, and sealing of the Holy Spirit. Have a time of silent prayer for confessing sins that keep you from being controlled by the Spirit.

Assignment

1. If you can obtain a copy of the booklet *My Heart, Christ's Home* by Robert Boyd Munger (InterVarsity Press), read it prayerfully. Ask God to show you changes you need to make in how you live your life.

2. Read chapter 6 of the text. Evaluate how much time you spend reading and studying God's Word each week. Also think about how Scripture has impacted your spiritual growth.

6
IMPACTED BY GOD'S WORD

Session Topic: Knowing and obeying God's Word are vital for spiritual maturity.

Icebreakers *(Choose one)*
1. Identify one specific way Scripture has changed your life.
2. In groups of two to five, prepare and present three-minute skits to show various ways people view Scripture and its relationship to everyday life.
3. Listen to the song "Thy Word" (Amy Grant, *Straight Ahead*, Myrrh).

Group Discovery Questions
1. What role does Scripture play in spiritual maturity?
2. Why is spiritual vitality dependent on "an abundant intake of Scripture"?
3. How should believers view sin? Why?
4. Read Acts 17:11 and 1 Thessalonians 2:13. How well do these verses describe you?
5. What is biblical meditation? How does it differ from popular concepts of meditation?
6. Read Matthew 7:24-27. Why isn't it sufficient just to know what God's Word says? What did Jesus say we need to do with Scripture? If we follow His instruction, what will result?

Personal Application Questions
1. How can we treasure God's Word in our hearts? (Ps. 119:11)
2. What are some specific ways you can meditate on God's Word this week?
3. How sufficient is your intake of God's Word for spiritual vitality? If it is not enough, what can you do to increase it?
4. How does your view of sin compare with that of the author of Psalm 119?
5. On a scale of 1 to 10, with 10 as highest, how would you

rate your obedience to God's Word?
6. In what area do you need to obey God's Word? How will you do so this week?

Optional Activities
1. Study Psalm 119. List the verbs that describe the psalmist's relation to God's Word. Summarize what you discover in a few sentences.
2. Investigate different methods of and resources for memorizing Scripture. (Have samples available for this meeting.) Choose one that is workable for you and begin to implement it this week.

Prayer Focus
Thank God for His Word and the way it has contributed to your spiritual maturity. Ask for His help to memorize it, meditate on it, and obey it this week. Pray Psalm 119:133.

Assignment
1. Using a concordance or *The Thompson Chain-Reference Bible*, locate several verses that relate to gaining victory over a temptation you are struggling with. Then memorize at least one this week.
2. Read chapter 7 of the text. Evaluate how wise you are in light of biblical teaching.

7
SPIRITUAL TRANSFORMATION

Session Topic: We become more mature through the wisdom imparted in Scripture by the Holy Spirit.

Icebreakers *(Choose one)*
1. Identify ways people seek to acquire wisdom today and evaluate the effectiveness of each.
2. Think of a believer, living or dead, who is or was wise. Briefly describe this person, telling why you chose him.
3. If you were a scientist and could make a truly wise person, what would he or she be like?

Group Discovery Questions
1. What is genuine wisdom?
2. Read Proverbs 1:20-33. Why does wisdom shout in the streets? What is wisdom's message? What will happen to those who ignore wisdom? To those who heed it?
3. Why can't we have real wisdom apart from knowing God through faith in His Son?
4. Answer each of the text author's catechism questions:
- Where can wisdom be found?
- What essentially identifies true wisdom?
- How valuable is wisdom?
- How is wisdom obtained?
- What are God's warnings about wisdom?
- What surprises are associated with wisdom?
- What should we do with wisdom?
5. Read James 3:13-18. What characterizes the wise person? The unwise person?
6. How does God's way of acquiring wisdom differ from man's attempts?

Personal Application Questions
1. How has your definition of wisdom changed as a result of this study?

2. Reread James 3:17. How much is each characteristic of wisdom present in your life?

3. Which characteristic of wisdom do you need to cultivate most? How can you do so this week?

4. What do you need to do to become more wise?

5. What do you usually do when you need wisdom in a situation? How do your actions compare with the four given at the end of the chapter?

6. Think of a specific time when you listened to the wisdom in God's Word. What happened as a result?

Optional Activities

1. Read Proverbs 1–9. Record what these chapters teach about wisdom. Organize your findings into categories, such as sources, characteristics, and results.

2. Using a concordance and/or topical Bible, find other verses that answer the seven catechism questions about wisdom. (See Group Discovery Question #4.)

3. Design a simple program to begin to teach children or teens to be wise.

Prayer Focus

Thank God for the wisdom He freely gives us in His Word and through prayer. Ask for His help and power to become a wise person.

Assignment

1. Memorize James 1:17.

2. Pray daily for wisdom to solve problems, improve relationships, deal with trials, etc.

3. Read chapter 8 of the textbook. Try to be aware of opportunities to serve others and of your initial responses to those needs.

8
THE FREEDOM OF SUBMISSION

Session Topic: Growing believers develop servant character qualities and serve others.

Icebreakers *(Choose one)*
1. Relate a time when someone served you. How did you react? How did you feel?
2. If you could nominate someone in your group or congregation as Servant of the Year, who would you select? Why? Prepare a brief nomination speech.

Group Discovery Questions
1. The author titled this chapter "The Freedom of Submission." Explain this seeming contradiction.
2. The author stated: "We distinguish ourselves as servants by whom we are becoming in character and by constancy of mature, Christian lifestyle rather than by the deeds we perform." Do you agree or disagree? Why?
3. What were the characteristics of the seven men chosen as servers in Acts 6:1-6? Why were these important qualities for serving?
4. Read 1 Timothy 3:8-13. What character qualities are church members to look for when selecting deacons and deaconesses or servants in general? Define/describe each quality.
5. How does one develop a servant's heart?
6. Why is servanthood a necessary characteristic of spiritual maturity?

Personal Application Questions
1. How has your concept of servanthood changed as a result of studying this chapter?
2. Review the characteristics of servants in Acts 6:1-6 and 1 Timothy 3:8-13. Which are present in your life?
3. Which of these servant characteristics do you most need to develop in your life? What practical steps can you take this

week to begin to do so?

4. Evaluate your effectiveness as a servant. Have you been emphasizing character or actions? Do you need to balance the two?

5. What practical, concrete ways can you serve others at home? At church? In your neighborhood? At work? In your community?

Optional Activities

1. Read or skim through the Book of Mark, focusing on Jesus as a servant. List His character qualities that made Him a model servant and ways He served others.

2. Write a newspaper want ad for a biblical servant.

3. Plan a servant day for your church. Brainstorm jobs that need to be done for people or around your building. Schedule a date and form committees to carry out your plan, such as publicity, equipment, and lunch/refreshments.

Prayer Focus

Thank God for the model servant, Jesus Christ. Ask God to help you become more like Him and to serve others with a willing attitude.

Assignment

1. Select one way to serve someone this week.

2. Read chapter 9 of the text. Think about what godly conduct entails.

3. Read one of these books on servanthood: *Serving One Another* by Gene A. Getz (Victor), *Improving Your Serve* by Charles R. Swindoll (Word), *He Humbled Himself* by Kenneth C. Fleming (Crossway).

9
BOTTOM LINE SPIRITUALITY

Session Topic: Spiritual character manifests itself in communion with God and godly character.

Icebreakers *(Choose one)*
1. Design a godly conduct medal for believers. Share it with your group members.
2. Describe the best time you had with God.

Group Discovery Questions
1. How do you know when you are on track with God?
2. Read Psalm 15. What does a genuine godly character look like? Give one or two concrete examples of each characteristic.
3. Why is it necessary to spend time in God's presence if we want to mature spiritually?
4. How does our speech reflect the degree of our spiritual maturity?
5. How does a godly person relate to unbelievers? To believers?
6. How does our character impact our testimony in our communities?
7. What are some of the results of communing with God and developing a godly character?

Personal Application Questions
1. How well are you living each of these three truths the textbook author summarized from Psalm 15?
• By way of concern, seeking God's holiness.
• By way of conduct, submitting to God's standards of holiness.
• By way of confidence, sojourning in the assurance of salvation brought about by habitually living out God's holiness.
2. If your friends and family were to judge your spiritual maturity by your speech, how would they rate you on a scale

of 1 to 10, with 10 as the highest?
3. How much time do you deliberately spend in God's presence? Do you need to increase it?
4. How well does your life match the godly characteristics listed in Psalm 15?
5. Which characteristic will you begin to develop or increase this week? How?
6. What kind of reputation do you have in your neighborhood and/or community? Is it pleasing to God?

Optional Activities
1. Review your schedule this past week. How much time did you spend in communion with God? How does it compare with other activities, such as watching TV or leisure reading? If you need to, schedule more time this week.
2. Paraphrase Psalm 15, making it personal for your present situation.

Prayer Focus
Thank God for His desire to be with you and to make you more like Him. Commit yourself to spending more time with Him and to living in accord with His Word.

Assignment
1. Write a letter to God describing your current spiritual character and asking for His help to align it more with His.
2. Read chapter 10 of the text. Draw as many parallels as you can between physical training and conditioning and spiritual training and conditioning.

10
SPIRITUAL CONDITIONING

Session Topic: Obeying the commands in 1 Thessalonians 5:14-22 conditions us for spiritual growth.

Icebreakers *(Choose one)*
1. Identify training rules that athletes have to keep. Relate each to spiritual training.
2. If you work out physically, tell what you do, why you do it, and what benefits you have gained. If you do not exercise, tell why you don't.

Group Discovery Questions
1. How does a believer get himself in peak condition spiritually?
2. Why is it necessary to exercise discipline and live by God's rules in order to mature spiritually?
3. Why are we mandated to overcome evil with good rather than seeking revenge?
4. How can we "be joyful always"?
5. What difference can a joyful, grateful attitude make in difficult situations?
6. What role does consistent prayer play in spiritual conditioning?
7. How do we "put out the Spirit's fire"? How can we guard against doing so?
8. Who are some contemporary examples of believers who "hold on to the good" and "avoid every kind of evil"? Why did you choose each one?

Personal Application Questions
1. How would your spouse or best friend describe your spiritual condition? Why?
2. How experienced are you in these four disciplines as described by the text author?
● Conditioning—holiness cultivation

- Skill—spiritual growth
- Obedience—biblical submission
- Focus—spiritual priority

3. Review the author's 10 events of Christian conditioning from 1 Thessalonians 5:14-22. What are two to three specific ways you can get involved in each?

4. Which events do you need to enter or get more involved in?

5. Who do you know who fits the category of spiritually needy? How can you minister to one of these people this week?

Optional Activities

1. Prepare and present skits to demonstrate how each or several of the 10 Christian conditioning events can be lived out.

2. Design a poster to encourage you to work out spiritually more consistently.

Prayer Focus

Ask God to help you obey the commands in 1 Thessalonians 5:14-22. Thank Him for the power of the Holy Spirit living in you to do so.

Assignment

1. Choose one command from 1 Thessalonians 5:14-22 that you need to obey. List several specific steps you will take to do so this week.

2. Read chapter 11 of the text. Define biblical unity in a sentence or two.

11
ONE-ANOTHER DIRECTIVES

Session Topic: Promoting biblical unity among believers by practicing the "one another" commands is evidence of spiritual maturity.

Icebreakers *(Choose one)*
1. Describe or do an activity that is easier to accomplish as a group than as an individual.
2. In groups of three to four, create a radio or TV commercial dealing with the concept of unity. Read or perform it for the rest of your group.

Group Discovery Questions
1. What are some examples of false unity that religious people are promoting today?
2. How can we promote unity among believers without compromising truth or sacrificing relationships?
3. Read John 17:11-23. What kind of unity did Jesus pray for? Why?
4. According to Philippians 2:1-8, how do we attain biblical unity? Give an example of each instruction. How does following Christ's example as a servant promote unity?
5. How does promoting unity contribute to spiritual maturity?
6. What do the "one another" commands tell you about Christian living?

Personal Application Questions
1. What are you doing to promote unity in your congregation? What else can you do?
2. Are you aware of any relational problems you are having with other believers that are disrupting unity? If so, what will you do about them?
3. Choose five or six "one another" commands listed in this chapter. How can you obey each one?

4. Which "one another" commands do you need to obey? Which one will you start with this week?

5. Would your fellow group or church members describe you as a peacemaker? Why or why not?

Optional Activities

1. Prepare a choral reading of 1 Corinthians 12:12-27. Divide this passage into body parts, such as arms, legs, trunk, hands, and feet. Omit the head since that is Christ's position. Include a few solo and entire group parts as well. Assign the solo parts. Then have your group stand in a body shape outlined on the floor with masking tape. Have everyone read the parts that correspond to where they are standing.

2. Select one of the "one another" commands. Find out what else Scripture says about that topic. For example, if you choose "honor one another" (Rom. 12:12), investigate other passages that deal with honoring others. Use a concordance and/or *The Thompson Chain-Reference Bible.*

3. Read Gene A. Getz's book *Building Up One Another* (Victor Books) for an in-depth study of 12 "one another" commands.

Prayer Focus

Praise God that He is the God who brings true unity and peace. Ask Him to help you promote unity without sacrificing truth.

Assignment

1. Memorize the verse that contains the "one another" command you chose to obey this week. Then practice it.

2. Read chapter 12 of the textbook. Evaluate how well you measure up to God's standards of spirituality.

12
MEASURING SPIRITUAL MATURITY

Session Topic: God states specific standards by which we can measure our spirituality.

Icebreakers *(Choose one)*
1. Respond: How do you react to tests? Why?
2. Identify a measuring device and tell what purpose it serves. Then discuss: Why do we use measuring devices? How do these reasons relate to God's measuring of our lives?

Group Discovery Questions
1. Summarize spirituality in a sentence or two.
2. Read Exodus 20:1-17. What specific tests for spirituality did God give us through Moses?
3. Read Matthew 5:3-12. What standards of spiritual maturity did Jesus propose?
4. According to 1 Corinthians 13:4-8a and Galatians 5:19-23, how did Paul measure spirituality?
5. What were Peter's standards for spiritual maturity? (2 Peter 1:3-9)
6. Compare the above five tests. What do they have in common? How do they differ from one another?
7. How can we be confident of passing God's final exam at the Judgment Seat of Christ?

Personal Application Questions
1. How do your standards of spiritual maturity compare with the five Scripture tests in this chapter?
2. Review each of the five passages that provide standards for measuring spirituality. Which of the qualities or actions are present in your life? Which are absent? What letter grade would you receive on this test?
3. How can Paul's attitude toward measuring up in Philippians 3:12-16 encourage you as you seek to become more like God?

4. What standard of spirituality do you fall short of the most? What will you do this week to begin to make it a part of your lifestyle?

Optional Activities

1. Using one or more of the five passages discussed, design a multiple choice, true-false, or other kind of test of spiritual maturity. Take it yourself. After this session, make copies to distribute to the rest of your group next week.

2. Read about the Judgment Seat of Christ in 1 Corinthians 3:10–4:5; and 2 Corinthians 5:10. On what basis will we be judged? What will we receive or forfeit as a result?

3. Conduct a talk show on the topic of measuring spiritual maturity. Have one or two group members each assume the roles of Moses, Jesus, Paul, and Peter and program host. Then discuss the biblical standards of spirituality.

Prayer Focus

Ask God for His help to measure up to His standards for our lives. Tell Him about your desire to pass His tests now and to have confidence in facing Him at the Judgment Seat of Christ.

Assignment

1. Meditate on one of the five standards passages each day this week.

2. Read chapter 13 and the Postscript of the textbook. Reflect on how much you have grown spiritually as a result of this study.

13
WHAT IF I FALL?

Session Topic: When we fail to obey God, He offers forgiveness if we repent of our sins.

Icebreakers *(Choose one)*
1. Describe a time when you felt like a failure. What made you feel that way? What did you do as a result? What other recourses did you have? What would you do differently if you could relive the situation?
2. Listen to the song "I Will Go On" (The Bill Gaither Trio, *Welcome Back Home,* Star Song). Discuss: What does this song teach about repentance?

Group Discovery Questions
1. Why do we tend to gloss over our sins instead of repenting as soon as we are aware of them? Why is this dangerous?
2. Read Psalm 51. What characterized David's repentance? Why are these characteristics necessary to receive God's forgiveness?
3. What specific changes did David experience after he repented?
4. To what did David recommit himself after he repented of his sin and his relationship with God was restored? Why did he do so?
5. How is David's psalm an encouragement to you?

Personal Application Questions
1. Generally, how honest are you with God about your sins? How does your level of honesty compare with David's in Psalm 51?
2. What excuses do people offer for their sins? Why? Which ones do you use?
3. How have your own experiences with sin, repentance, and restoration to God paralleled David's as recorded in Psalm 51?

4. What sins do you need to repent of and receive God's forgiveness for? Will you do so now?

5. How much has spiritual maturity become a greater priority in your life the past few weeks?

6. How have you grown spiritually as a result of reading this book and participating in these sessions?

Optional Activities

1. Write a psalm about a recent time when you sinned, repented, and experienced God's forgiveness.

2. Study Psalm 32, the sequel to Psalm 51. What do you learn about repentance and its results?

3. Review what you learned about spiritual maturity from this study. Then create a commercial or print ad promoting it. Share it with your group.

Prayer Focus

Silently confess any known sins to God; be specific. Then thank Him for His forgiveness when you sin. Verbally pray one of Paul's prayers included in the Postscript of the text.

Assignment

1. Thank God for the insights and challenges He gave you in this study and continue to ask for His help to become more like Him.

2. Each day this week, pray one of Paul's prayers for spiritual growth for your group members or other believers you know.

ENDNOTES

INTRODUCTION
1. Emily E.S. Elliott, "Thou Didst Leave Thy Throne," stanza 5.
2. Richard Mayhue, *Spiritual Intimacy* (Wheaton, Illinois: Victor Books, 1990).

PART ONE—"GOD'S PLAN"
1. J.C. Ryle, *Holiness* (Old Tappan, New Jersey: Fleming H. Revell, rpt., n.d.), vii.

ONE
1. Charles Wesley, "And Can It Be?" stanza 1.

TWO
1. Charles Wesley, "Love Divine, All Loves Excelling," stanza 4.
2. Richard F. Lovelace, "Evangelical Spirituality: A Church Historian's Perspective" in *Journal of the Evangelical Theological Society*, 31:1 (March 1988) 33.
3. John Brown, *The First Epistle of Peter*, v. 1 (Edinburgh: The Banner of Truth Trust, rpt., n.d.), 106.
4. John Owen, *The Holy Spirit: His Gift and Power* (Grand Rapids: Kregel Publications, rpt., 1954), 230.
5. Amy Carmichael, *IF* (Grand Rapids: Zondervan Publishing House, rpt., 1980).

THREE
1. Walter Chalmers Smith, "Immortal, Invisible," stanza 1.

FOUR
1. Ancient Irish hymn of unknown authorship, "Be Thou My Vision," stanza 1.
2. Jerry Bridges, *The Practice of Godliness* (Colorado Springs: NavPress, 1983), 69.

FIVE
1. Edwin Hatch, "Breathe on Me, Breath of God," stanzas 1 and 2.
2. This chapter does not intend to deal with the issues commonly associated with pentecostal, charismatic, and Third Wave tradition. For a complete biblical treatment of these areas, please consult John MacArthur, Jr., *Charismatic Chaos* (Grand Rapids: Zondervan Publishing House, 1992) and Richard Mayhue, *Divine Healing Today* (Winona Lake, Indiana: BMH Books, 1983).

SIX
1. John Burton, "Holy Bible, Book Divine," stanzas 1 and 2.
2. John F. MacArthur, Jr., *Our Sufficiency in Christ* (Dallas: Word Publishing, 1991), 261.
3. As background material for this study, refer to Richard Mayhue, *Spiritual Intimacy* (Wheaton: Victor Books, 1990), chapter 2 "Listening to God" and chapter 3 "Thinking Like God." Also see Richard Mayhue,

How to Interpret the Bible for Yourself (Winona Lake, Indiana: BMH Books, 1986).

4. John Owen, *Thinking Spiritually* (London: Grace Publication Trust, rpt., 1989), 21-22.

5. For a fuller discussion see Willem A. Van Gemeren, "Psalms" in *The Expositor's Bible Commentary,* v. 5 (Grand Rapids: Zondervan Publishing House, 1991), 737-38.

6. My favorite helps to make this a reality are (1) *The Daily Walk,* published monthly by Walk Thru the Bible Ministries, which can be purchased at your local church bookstore or ordered by writing to *The Daily Walk,* P.O. Box 478, Mt. Morris, IL 61504 and (2) *The One Year Bible* (Wheaton, Illinois: Tyndale House, 1986).

7. Ruth Harms Calkins, *Lord I Keep Running Back to You* (Wheaton, Illinois: Tyndale House, 1979), 82-83.

SEVEN
1. Thomas O. Chisholm, "O to Be Like Thee!" stanza 1.
2. Henry Beach and Roy McKie, *Sailing: A Sailor's Dictionary* (New York: Workman Publishing, 1981), cover.

EIGHT
1. Fanny J. Crosby, "I Am Thine, O Lord," stanza 2.

NINE
1. Reginald Heber, "Holy, Holy, Holy," stanza 1.
2. Used by permission.

PART TWO—"THE CHRISTIAN'S PRACTICE"
1. William Wilberforce, *Real Christianity* (Portland: Multnomah Press, 1982), 125.

TEN
1. John H. Sammis, "Trust and Obey," stanza 5.

ELEVEN
1. Sabine Baring-Gould, "Onward, Christian Soldiers," stanza 3.

TWELVE
1. Horatio G. Spafford, "It Is Well with My Soul," stanza 1.
2. Phillip Keller, *A Shepherd Looks at Psalm 23* (Grand Rapids: Zondervan Publishing House, 1970), 30.

THIRTEEN
1. Bernard of Clairvaux, "Jesus, the Very Thought of Thee," stanza 3.

POSTSCRIPT
1. Isaac Watts, "When I Survey the Wondrous Cross," stanza 4.
2. William R. Featherstone, "My Jesus, I Love Thee," stanza 3.